COOKING
MEASURE FOR MEASURE

All the flavor of regular salt, but only half the sodium.

Creative cookery, with a detailed breakdown of nutrient information for each recipe.

Sixteen days of complete menus.

It's all part of this new MORTON LITE SALT® COOKBOOK: COOKING MEASURE FOR MEASURE. Over 250 recipes show you how to use Morton Lite Salt mixture as regular table salt in cooking, baking and at-the-table seasoning.

Everything from appetizers to meats to casseroles to desserts is highlighted in this 224 page book. Following each recipe, nutrient information is provided on calories, protein, carbohydrates, fats, sodium, potassium and cholesterol. Plus, there's a comprehensive chart listing sodium, potassium and calorie content of popular foods.

The Morton Lite Salt Cookbook

COOKING MEASURE FOR MEASURE

by Frani Shaver Lauda

POPULAR LIBRARY • NEW YORK

CONTENTS

What hymns are sung, what praises said
  for homemade miracles of bread. . . .

and other simple but savory fare.

Salt and flavor are almost synonymous with Morton Salt Company, whose little umbrella girl has meant good taste in cooking and at the table for more than a century.

Today, the Morton Salt girl has another fine product for you—Morton Lite Salt, a salt and potassium chloride mixture, the first iodized salt with all the flavor but only half the sodium of regular table salt. Morton Lite Salt is used measure-for-measure in place of regular salt for cooking, baking and at-the-table seasoning.

In recommending this book to you, we remind you that Morton Lite Salt contains sodium and is not a salt substitute. It is not for persons on a sodium or potassium-restricted diet. It's a new way to salt for normal, healthy people.

For your enjoyment, we've developed a collection of recipes kitchen-tested for flavor with Morton Lite Salt. From appetizers through desserts, from everyday through a touch of gourmet, we hope you and your family will like this taste-tempting selection. We've also included daily menu suggestions for each season.

Unique to this cookbook . . . each recipe has been evaluated by a computerized nutrient data bank to determine its per-serving values for the following nutrients: calories, carbohydrates, protein, fats, sodium, potassium and cholesterol. These values are listed immediately after each recipe for your information and convenience.

Bon appetit!

Frani Shaver Lauda

Frani Shaver Lauda

CHAPTER 1

SODIUM/POTASSIUM/ CALORIE COUNTER

CHAPTER 1

SODIUM/POTASSIUM/CALORIE COUNTER

The following chart has been prepared to show the amounts of sodium, potassium and calories contained in the various foods we consume. The figures listed are based on the average portions of these foods commonly eaten.

Meat and Poultry*	Portion	Sodium (mg.)	Potassium (mg.)	Calories
Bacon	1 strip (1 oz.)	71	16	156
Beef				
Corned beef (canned)	3 slices	803	51	184
Hamburger	¼ lb.	41	382	224
Pot roast (rump)	½ lb.	43	309	188
Sirloin steak	½ lb.	57	545	260
Chicken (broiler)	3½ oz.	78	320	151
Duck	3½ oz.	82	285	326
Frankfurter (beef)	⅛ lb.	550	110	129
Ham				
Fresh	¼ lb.	37	260	126
Cured, butt	¼ lb.	518	239	123
Cured, shank	¼ lb.	336	155	91
Lamb				
Shoulder chop	½ lb.	72	422	260
Rib chops (2)	½ lb.	68	398	238
Leg roast	¼ lb.	41	246	96

* Before cooking.

	Portion	Sodium (mg.)	Potassium (mg.)	Calories
Meat and Poultry*				
Liver				
Beef	3½ oz.	86	325	136
Calf	3½ oz.	131	436	141
Pork				
Loin chop	6 oz.	52	500	314
Spareribs (3 or 4)	3½ oz.	51	360	209
Sausage (link or bulk)	3½ oz.	740	140	450
Bologna	3½ oz.	1300	230	304
Turkey	3½ oz.	40	320	268
Veal				
Cutlet	6 oz.	46	448	235
Loin chop	½ lb.	54	384	514
Rump roast	¼ lb.	36	244	84
Fish				
Clams (4 large, 9 small)	3½ oz.	36	235	82
Cod	3½ oz.	70	382	78
Crabmeat	3½ oz.	500	265	100
Flounder or Sole	3½ oz.	56	366	68
Lobster (boiled with 2 tbsp. butter)	¾ lb.	210	180	308
Oysters (5 to 8)				
Fresh	3½ oz.	73	121	66
Frozen	3½ oz.	380	210	66
Salmon (pink, canned)	3½ oz.	387	361	141
Sardines (8, canned in oil)	3½ oz.	510	560	311
Shrimp	3½ oz.	140	220	91
Tuna (canned in oil)	3½ oz.	800	301	288
(canned in water)	3½ oz.	41	279	127
Dairy Products, Margarine				
Butter, salted	1 pat	99	2	72
Butter, unsalted	1 pat	1	2	72
Cheese				
American, Cheddar	1 oz.	197	23	112
American, processed	1 oz.	318	22	107
Cottage, creamed	3½ oz.	229	85	106
Cream, heavy	1 tbsp.	35	10	52
Egg	1 large	66	70	88

*Before cooking.

Dairy Products	Portion	Sodium (mg.)	Potassium (mg.)	Calories
Ice cream				
Chocolate	½ pint	75	**	300
Vanilla	½ pint	82	210	290
Milk				
Whole	8 oz.	122	352	159
Skim	8 oz.	130	370	75
Buttermilk	8 oz.	530	410	90
Margarine				
Salted	1 pat	99	2	72
Unsalted	1 tbsp.	0	0	100
Breads, Cereals, etc.				
Bread				
Rye	1 slice	128	33	56
Enriched white	1 slice	117	20	62
Whole wheat	1 slice	121	63	56
Cereals (ready-to-eat)				
Corn flakes	1 cup	165	40	95
Bran flakes	1 cup	920	730	350
Puffed rice, wheat	1 cup	22	229	60
Macaroni, enriched, cooked tender	1 cup	1	85	151
Noodles, enriched, cooked	1 cup	3	70	200
Oatmeal, cooked	1 cup	1	130	148
Pancake, 4-in. diam.	1	425	100	230
Rice, white, dry	¼ cup	3	45	178
Spaghetti, enriched, cooked tender	1 cup	2	92	166
Waffles, enriched	1 waffle	356	109	209
Wheat germ	3 tbsp.	1	232	102
Fruits*				
Apple	1 medium	1	165	87
Apricots				
Fresh	2-3	1	281	51
Canned in syrup	3 halves	1	234	86
Dried	17 halves	26	979	260
Avocado	½	343	340	170
Banana	1, 6-in.	1	370	85
Blueberries	1 cup	1	81	62
Cantaloupe	¼ melon	12	251	30
Cherries				
Fresh	½ cup	2	191	58
Canned in syrup	½ cup	1	124	89

* All portions weigh 3½ oz. unless otherwise noted.
**Data not available.

13

	Portion	Sodium (mg.)	Potassium (mg.)	Calories
Fruits*				
Dates				
Fresh	10 medium	1	648	274
Dried pitted	1 cup (6 oz.)	2	1150	488
Fruit cocktail	½ cup	5	161	76
Grapefruit	½ medium	1	135	41
Grapes	22	3	158	69
Orange	1 small	1	200	49
Peaches				
Fresh	1 medium	1	202	38
Canned	2 halves, 2 tbsp. syrup	2	130	78
Pears				
Fresh	½ pear	2	130	61
Canned	2 halves, 2 tbsp. syrup	1	84	76
Pineapple				
Fresh	¾ cup	1	146	52
Canned	1 slice and syrup	1	96	74
Plums				
Fresh	2 medium	2	299	66
Canned	3 medium, 2 tbsp. syrup	1	142	83
Prunes				
Dried	10 large	8	694	255
Strawberries	10 large	1	164	37
Watermelon	½ cup	1	100	26
Vegetables				
Artichoke				
Base and soft end of leaves	1 large bud	30	301	44
Asparagus				
Fresh	⅔ cup	1	183	20
Canned	6 spears	271	191	21
Beans, baked	⅝ cup	2	704	159
Beans, canned with pork	½ cup	200	704	159
Beans, green				
Fresh	1 cup	5	189	31
Canned	1 cup	295	109	30
Beans, lima				
Fresh	⅝ cup	1	422	111
Canned	½ cup	271	255	110
Frozen	⅝ cup	129	394	118

*All portions weigh 3½ oz. unless otherwise noted.

	Portion	Sodium (mg.)	Potassium (mg.)	Calories
Vegetables				
Beets				
Fresh	½ cup	36	172	27
Canned	½ cup	196	138	31
Broccoli, fresh	⅔ cup	10	267	26
Brussels sprouts	6-7 medium	10	273	36
Cabbage				
Raw, shredded	1 cup	20	233	24
Cooked	⅗ cup	14	163	20
Carrots				
Raw	1 large	47	341	42
Cooked	⅔ cup	33	222	31
Canned	⅔ cup	236	120	30
Cauliflower	⅞ cup	9	206	22
Celery	1 outer or 3 inner stalks	63	170	8
Corn				
Fresh	1 medium ear	trace	196	100
Canned	½ cup	196	81	70
Cucumber, pared	½ medium	3	80	7
Lettuce, iceberg	3½ oz.	9	264	14
Mushrooms, uncooked	10 small, 4 large	15	414	28
Onions, uncooked	1 medium	10	157	38
Peas				
Fresh	⅔ cup	1	196	71
Canned	¾ cup	236	96	88
Frozen	3½ oz.	115	135	68
Potatoes				
Boiled (in skin)	1 medium	3	407	76
French fried	10 pieces	3	427	137
Radishes	10 small	18	322	17
Sauerkraut	⅔ cup	747	140	18
Spinach	½ cup	45	291	21
Tomatoes				
Raw	1 medium	4	366	33
Canned	½ cup	130	217	21
Paste	3½ oz.	38	888	82

Note: Because vegetable counts vary greatly from raw to cooked state, values are for cooked vegetables with no added salt unless otherwise noted. Frozen vegetables have virtually the same count as fresh vegetables, when cooked, unless otherwise noted.

	Portion	Sodium (mg.)	Potassium (mg.)	Calories
Beverages				
Apple juice	6 oz.	2	187	87
Beer	8 oz.	8	46	114
Coca-Cola	6 oz.	2	88	78
Coffee (brewed)	1 cup	3	149	5
Decaffeinated	1 cup	1–6	80	0
Cranberry cocktail	7 oz.	2	20	130
Ginger ale	8 oz.	18	1	80
Grape juice	3½ oz.	1	120	66
Lemon juice	3½ oz.	1	130	25
Orange juice				
Canned	8 oz.	3	500	120
Fresh	8 oz.	3	496	111
Prune juice	6 oz.	4	423	138
Tea	8 oz.	2	21	2
Whiskey, etc.	1 oz.	1	trace	90
Wine, table	3½ oz.	4–7	20–120	60–120
Snacks, Miscellaneous				
Candy				
Chocolate creams	1 candy	1	15	51
Milk chocolate	1 oz.	30	105	152
Mayonnaise	1 tbsp.	117	9	119
Nuts				
Cashews, roasted	6-8	2	84	84
Peanuts, roasted				
Salted	1 tbsp.	69	105	85
Unsalted	1 tbsp.	trace	111	86
Peanut butter	1 tbsp.	100	110	95
Oil, vegetable	1 tbsp.	0	0	144
Olives				
Green	2 medium	312	7	15
Ripe	2 large	150	5	37
Potato chips	5 chips	34	88	54
Pretzels, 3 ring	1 average	87	7	12
Salt, Morton Lite	¼ tsp.	275	366	0
Salt, regular	¼ tsp.	622	0	0
Salt, substitute	¼ tsp.	0	698	0
Saltines	1 oz.	450	30	100

SOURCES

Church, C. F. and Church, H. N., *Food Values of Portions Commonly Used*, 11th ed. Philadelphia: J. B. Lippincott Co., 1970.

Gormican, A., *Inorganic Elements in Foods Used in Hospital Menus*, *J. Am. Diet. Assoc.* 56:397-403, May, 1970.

CHAPTER 2

MENUS

CHAPTER 2

MENUS

In the following suggested menus, we have starred the recipes given in this book. To find them, consult the index.

SPRING

DAY 1

BREAKFAST

Grapefruit juice
Shredded wheat
Toast, selected margarine[1]
    and currant jelly
Skim or low-fat milk
Coffee or tea

LUNCH

Lemon-Broiled Chicken*
Rice with Sage*
Italian Carrot and Zucchini
    Salad*
Home-Style Pear Pie*
Skim or low-fat milk
Coffee or tea

DINNER

Beef Carbonnade*
Poppyseed Noodles*
Green Beans*
Pink Grapefruit Salad*
All Whole-Wheat Bread*
    with selected margarine
Silver Cake with White
    Mountain Frosting*
Coffee or tea

DAY 2

BREAKFAST

Orange sections
Hot wheat cereal
English muffin, selected
    margarine and plum jam
Skim or low-fat milk
Coffee or tea

[1] Where margarine is indicated, use unsalted polyunsaturated margarine.

19

LUNCH

Chef's Salad with True
  Italian Dressing* (make
  Good Green Salad,* add-
  ing strips of chicken, Swiss
  cheese and lean beef)
Sesame Twists*
Cherry Cobbler*
Skim or low-fat milk
Coffee or tea

DINNER

Roast Lamb* with mint jelly
Mashed Potatoes*
Asparagus Polonaise*
Tomato Aspic*
Parkerhouse rolls with
  selected margarine
Lemon Chiffon Pie*
Coffee or tea

DAY 3

BREAKFAST

Cantaloupe
Puffed wheat
Cinnamon toast
Skim or low-fat milk
Coffee or tea

LUNCH

Jellied Gazpacho*
Shrimp salad sandwich
Canned plums
Skim or low-fat milk
Coffee or tea

DINNER

Beef and Rice Skillet Dinner*
Zucchini*
Jellied Waldorf Salad*
Club rolls with selected
  margarine
Apricot Skillet Cake*
Coffee or tea

DAY 4

BREAKFAST

Strawberries
Canadian bacon
Toast and selected margarine
Skim or low-fat milk
Coffee or tea

LUNCH

Broiled Fish Fillets with
  Sesame*
Basque Potatoes*
Chinese Slaw*
Soft rolls with selected
  margarine
Date and Nut Bars*
Skim or low-fat milk
Coffee or tea

DINNER

Lamb Stew*
Boiled Potatoes*
Perfection Salad*
Bread sticks with selected
  margarine
Broiled Bananas with Sour
  Cream*
Coffee or tea

SUMMER

DAY 1

BREAKFAST

Orange juice
Blueberry pancakes with
  selected margarine and
  syrup
Skim or low-fat milk
Coffee or tea

LUNCH

Salad: Cottage cheese and
  fruits in season with Citrus
  Honey Dressing*

Melba toast and selected
  margarine
Oatmeal Fudge Cookies*
Iced tea

DINNER

Broiled Lamb Chops*
Spaghetti with Eggplant
  Sauce*
Good Green Salad* with
  True Italian Dressing*
Pumpernickel bread with
  selected margarine
Yellow Cake* with California
  Orange Sauce*
Coffee or tea

DAY 2

BREAKFAST

Raspberries
Soft-cooked egg
Toast and selected margarine
Skim or low-fat milk
Coffee or tea

LUNCH

Sliced cold roast veal
Macaroni Salad, Italian
  Style*
Sliced tomatoes and
  cucumbers
Strawberry Snow*
Skim or low-fat milk
Coffee or tea

DINNER

Quick Gazpacho*
Baked Chicken with Grapes*
Really Good Rice*
Fruit salad: Fresh peaches
  and blueberries with Pink
  Poppyseed Dressing*

Thin rye crackers with
  selected margarine
Maple-Baked Pears*
Coffee or tea

DAY 3

BREAKFAST

Quarter honeydew
English muffin with peanut
  butter and grape jelly
Skim or low-fat milk
Coffee or tea

LUNCH

Jellied Orange Chicken
  Salad*
Poppyseed rolls and selected
  margarine
Vanilla yogurt with sliced
  fresh peaches
Coffee or tea

DINNER

Chili Pear Broil*
Armenian Ground Lamb
  Kabobs*
Mexican Style Corn*
Curried Rice*
Celery fans
Vanilla Trifle*
Coffee or tea

DAY 4

BREAKFAST

Corn flakes and strawberries
Toast, selected margarine and
  orange marmalade
Skim or low-fat milk
Coffee or tea

LUNCH

Hungarian Goulash*
Noodles*

Sliced tomatoes with Sweet
  Mayonnaise Dressing*
Banana
Skim or low-fat milk
Coffee or tea

DINNER
Baked Whole Fish in Foil*
Baked Potato*
Grapefruit and Mushroom
  Salad*
Cherry tomatoes
Bran muffins and selected
  margarine
Molded Summer Fruit*
Coffee or tea

FALL

DAY 1

BREAKFAST
Puffed wheat with sliced
  banana
Toast, selected margarine and
  grape jelly
Skim or low-fat milk
Coffee or tea

LUNCH
Tomato stuffed with chicken
  salad
Party-size rye bread and
  selected margarine
Honeydew Tropicale*
Skim or low-fat milk
Coffee or tea

DINNER
Spiced Garbanzos*
Apple-Stuffed Veal Rolls*
Poppyseed Noodles*
Good Green Salad* with
  Tomato Salad Dressing*
Cherry Pie*
Coffee or tea

DAY 2

BREAKFAST
Half grapefruit, broiled
One egg, scrambled
Toast, selected margarine
  and cherry preserves
Skim or low-fat milk
Coffee or tea

LUNCH
Halibut Steak Jardinière*
Really Good Rice*
Apple Crisp*
Skim or low-fat milk
Coffee or tea

DINNER
Old-Fashioned Stuffed
  Cabbage*
Mashed Turnips* and
  potatoes
Dilled Cucumber Slices*
Rye bread and selected
  margarine
Streusel Coffee Cake*
Coffee or tea

DAY 3

BREAKFAST
Unsweetened pineapple-
  grapefruit juice
French toast and honey
Skim or low-fat milk
Coffee or tea

LUNCH
Slim-line Beef Patties* on a
  bun with selected marga-
  rine and Sweet Catsup
  Sauce*
Potato Salad*
Radishes
Easy Apple-Noodle Bake*
Skim or low-fat milk
Coffee or tea

DINNER

Chicken Piccata*
Noodles* with selected
   margarine
Chinese-Style Cabbage*
Fruit salad: Pears, halved red
   grapes and oranges
Poppyseed Dressing*
Oatmeal Batter Bread* and
   selected margarine
Orange sherbet
Austrian Crescents*
Coffee or tea

DAY 4

BREAKFAST

Two tangerines
Pancakes, selected marga-
   rine and syrup
Skim or low-fat milk
Coffee or tea

LUNCH

Deviled egg
Old-Fashioned Macaroni
   Salad*
Sliced tomato
Fruit Juice Snow*
Skim or low-fat milk
Coffee or tea

DINNER

Oatmeal Meat Loaf
   Neapolitan*
Mashed Potatoes*
Italian-Style Green Beans*
Jellied Orange and Apple
   Salad (see Invent-Your-
   Own Jellied Fruit Salad*)
Hot garlic bread (made with
   selected margarine)
Canned pineapple rings
Almond Squares*
Coffee or tea

WINTER

DAY 1

BREAKFAST

Stewed apricots
Hot oatmeal
English muffins with
   selected margarine
Skim or low-fat milk
Coffee or tea

LUNCH

Tarragon-Broiled
   Hamburger*
Spanish Rice*
Cole slaw
Canned pears
Skim or low-fat milk
Coffee or tea

DINNER

Fish Steaks Provençal*
Boiled Potatoes* with marga-
   rine and parsley
Broccoli Florentine*
Cucumber slices in Basic
   French Dressing*
Poppyseed Batter Bread*
   with selected margarine
Buttermilk Lemon Sherbet*
Coffee or tea

DAY 2

BREAKFAST

Half grapefruit
Puffed rice
Toast with selected margarine
   and jam
Skim or low-fat milk
Coffee or tea

LUNCH

Sandwich: Swiss cheese on
   rye with selected marga-

23

rine, lettuce and Hot
Mustard Sauce, Dijon
Style*
Sliced tomato
Old-Fashioned Doughnut*
Skim or low-fat milk
Coffee or tea

DINNER
Chicken with Peaches*
Green Peas à la Française*
Golden Rice*
Good Green Salad*
Hot French bread and
selected margarine
Canned Royal Anne cherries
Coffee or tea

DAY 3

BREAKFAST
Orange juice
Toast and peanut butter
Skim or low-fat milk
Coffee or tea

LUNCH
Beef-Vegetable Soup*
Onion Bread Rounds* with
selected margarine
Pineapple Whip*
Butterscotch Brownies*
Skim or low-fat milk
Coffee or tea

DINNER
Roast Pork* with apple
sauce
Spiced Red Cabbage*

Mashed Potatoes*
Dilled Cucumber Slices*
Popovers* with selected
margarine
Banana Fruit Cups* with
Spirited Syrup*
Coffee or tea

DAY 4

BREAKFAST
Stewed prunes
Cream of rice cereal
Toast with selected margarine
and strawberry jam
Skim or low-fat milk
Coffee or tea

LUNCH
Sandwich: Chicken, sliced
tomatoes, lettuce, selected
margarine, Sweet Mayon-
naise Dressing* on Good
White Bread*
Pineapple Relish Mold*
Skim or low-fat milk
Coffee or tea

DINNER
Savory Meat Loaf*
Baked Potatoes*
Dilly Beans and Carrots*
Sesame Pears*
Celery, Radishes
Flaky Biscuits* with selected
margarine
Angel Food Cake* with
thawed frozen raspberries
Coffee or tea

CHAPTER 3

APPETIZERS, SOUPS AND RELISHES

CHAPTER 3

APPETIZERS, SOUPS AND RELISHES

Though the foods in this chapter are not served every day, they are part of every good cook's stock in trade.

When you entertain friends, it's nice to provide snacks (hors d'oeuvres) to accompany liquid refreshment. Try the appetizers included here.

Good soups have many functions. At company meals a homemade soup can set the stage for what's ahead. When the family dinner is a bit late, a mug of soup in the kitchen comforts Dad and the youngsters without destroying appetites. Hearty soups can serve as a lunch or supper, since many contain both meat and vegetables. Soup adds a pleasant hot touch to sandwich meals. Homemade beef, chicken or turkey broth on hand in the refrigerator or freezer is a quick and easy stepping stone to many delicious recipes.

Read on for other tasty mealtime accompaniments, pungent relishes and spicy fruit go-alongs. Ideal for company, they are also a real treat for "just the family."

PICKLED MUSHROOMS

1 lb. fresh mushrooms
1¼ cups cider vinegar
⅓ cup water
1 tablespoon instant minced onion
1½ teaspoons Morton Lite Salt mixture
½ teaspoon coarse-ground black pepper
2 bay leaves
6 to 8 celery leaves
2 sprigs parsley, or 1 tablespoon parsley flakes

Wash mushrooms, pat dry and trim off stem ends. Cut large mushrooms in half. Place in bowl. In a small saucepan, combine remaining ingredients. Bring to a boil; reduce heat and simmer for 5 minutes. Pour over mushrooms; cool. Spoon mushrooms and marinade into a 1-quart jar with a tight cover. Refrigerate 24 hours before serving. Makes 1 quart.

Per Recipe

Calories	410	Sodium	1783 mg.
Carbohydrate	93 Gm.	Potassium	4200 mg.
Protein	19 Gm.	Cholesterol	0
Fat	3 Gm.		

MARINATED ARTICHOKE HEARTS

2 packages (9 oz. each) frozen artichoke hearts
¾ cup vegetable oil
⅓ cup tarragon vinegar
2 tablespoons finely chopped parsley
1 tablespoon finely chopped onion
1 teaspoon dry mustard
½ teaspoon Morton Lite Salt mixture
¼ teaspoon pepper
1 clove garlic, minced

Cook artichoke hearts following package directions for minimum cooking period, crisp-tender. Drain. Meanwhile, mix remaining ingredients in medium bowl. Add artichoke hearts and toss. Cover and refrigerate overnight. Serve chilled. (Artichokes may also be heated in the marinade and served from a fondue pot or chafing dish held over low heat.) Serve with wooden picks. Makes about 60, enough for 10.

Per Serving

Calories	161	Sodium	67 mg.
Carbohydrate	2 Gm.	Potassium	87 mg.
Protein	trace	Cholesterol	0
Fat	17 Gm.		

VEGETABLE ANTIPASTO

⅔ cup white vinegar
⅔ cup vegetable oil
2 tablespoons instant minced onion
1 teaspoon Italian seasoning
1 teaspoon Morton Lite Salt mixture
1 teaspoon sugar
¼ teaspoon instant minced garlic

⅛ teaspoon coarse-ground black pepper
1 can (14 oz.) artichoke hearts, drained and halved
1 can (6 to 8 oz.) sliced mushrooms, drained
1 can (7¼ oz.) baby carrots, drained
1 jar (2½ oz.) pitted ripe olives, drained

In a small saucepan, combine vinegar, oil and seasonings. Bring to boiling point. Cool slightly. Mix vegetables in a bowl. Add marinade and toss to coat. Cover and refrigerate at least 12 hours, or overnight. Makes 1 quart.

Per Recipe

Calories	1086	Sodium	2513 mg.
Carbohydrate	188 Gm.	Potassium	4500 mg.
Protein	29 Gm.	Cholesterol	0
Fat	34 Gm.		

SPICED GARBANZOS

1 tablespoon instant minced
  onion
1 tablespoon water
1 can (1 lb. 4 oz.) chick peas
  (garbanzos), drained

¼ teaspoon pepper
⅛ teaspoon Morton Lite Salt
  mixture
Dash garlic powder

In a small bowl, mix onion with water and let stand 10
minutes. Add remaining ingredients; toss gently. Chill.
Makes 2 cups.

Per Recipe

Calories	2283	Sodium	346 mg.
Carbohydrate	403 Gm.	Potassium	250 mg.
Protein	122 Gm.	Cholesterol	0
Fat	28 Gm.		

RAW VEGETABLE MEDLEY

1 small head cauliflower
2 medium carrots
1 bunch radishes
2 bunches green onions

1 medium zucchini
3 stalks celery
Mustard Dill Dip
Celery Seed Dip

Cut cauliflower into flowerets. Wash and drain on paper
towel. Peel carrots and slice thin on the diagonal. Rinse
and drain. Trim radishes and wash well. Make into roses
and crisp in ice water. Trim off root ends of green onions
and peel off outer layer. Trim so 2 inches of green remain.
Rinse in cold water. Trim off ends of zucchini and scrub
under cold water. Cut in half lengthwise, then cut into
strips about ½ inch square and 3 inches long. Crisp in ice
water. Trim ends from celery and cut each stalk into
half-inch strips about 3 inches long. Rinse and drain. Arrange all these vegetables on a platter in a pleasing design,
garnishing if desired with parsley or curly endive. Serve
with Mustard Dill Dip and Celery Seed Dip. Serves 10.

Per Serving

Calories	21	Sodium	31 mg.
Carbohydrate	5 Gm.	Potassium	100 mg.
Protein	1 Gm.	Cholesterol	0
Fat	trace		

MUSTARD DILL DIP

1 cup dairy sour cream
1 teaspoon prepared mustard
1 teaspoon dill weed

½ teaspoon Morton Lite Salt mixture
½ teaspoon prepared horseradish (optional)

Combine all ingredients in small bowl, stirring until well mixed. Chill at least 6 hours or overnight. Makes 1 cup.

Per Recipe

Calories	458	Sodium	711 mg.
Carbohydrate	8 Gm.	Potassium	800 mg.
Protein	7 Gm.	Cholesterol	152 mg.
Fat	44 Gm.		

CELERY SEED DIP

1 cup dairy sour cream
1 teaspoon celery seed

½ teaspoon Morton Lite Salt mixture
½ teaspoon dry mustard

Combine all ingredients and stir until well mixed. Chill at least 6 hours or overnight. Makes 1 cup.

Per Recipe

Calories	454	Sodium	646 mg.
Carbohydrate	8 Gm.	Potassium	*
Protein	7 Gm.	Cholesterol	152 mg.
Fat	43 Gm.		

* Data not available.

AVOCADO DIP

2 tablespoons instant minced onion
2 tablespoons water
2 ripe avocados, peeled and pitted
¼ cup diced tomato
¼ cup mayonnaise
3 tablespoons lemon juice
2 teaspoons chili powder
1¼ teaspoons Morton Lite Salt mixture
½ teaspoon coarse-ground black pepper
¼ teaspoon garlic powder

Mix onion with water and let stand 10 minutes. Mash avocado in small mixing bowl. Add onion along with remaining ingredients; mix well. Serve with vegetable relishes. Makes about 2 cups.

Per Recipe

Calories	1031	Sodium	1402 mg.
Carbohydrate	31 Gm.	Potassium	2800 mg.
Protein	9 Gm.	Cholesterol	40 mg.
Fat	102 Gm.		

BAKED STUFFED MUSHROOMS

8 to 10 large fresh mushrooms
⅓ cup dry bread crumbs
2 tablespoons chopped walnuts
2 teaspoons dry minced chives
1 teaspoon parsley flakes
½ teaspoon paprika
½ teaspoon Morton Lite Salt mixture
⅛ teaspoon pepper
2 tablespoons half-and-half
Vegetable oil

Wash mushrooms, trim stems, then remove stems. Lay caps aside and chop stems. Combine the chopped stems with bread crumbs, walnuts, chives, parsley, paprika, salt and pepper. Add half-and-half; toss with a fork to moisten all ingredients. Brush mushroom caps inside and out with vegetable oil. Fill each mushroom cap with crumb mixture. Drizzle with vegetable oil, using about ⅛ teaspoon for each mushroom. Place in a greased 9-inch-square pan. Bake at 400° for 20 minutes, or until mushroom caps are just tender and crumb mixture is lightly browned. Serve immediately. Serves 4.

Calories	108	Sodium	202 mg.
Carbohydrate	9 Gm.	Potassium	425 mg.
Protein	3 Gm.	Cholesterol	6 mg.
Fat	7 Gm.		

HOMEMADE POPCORN

3 tablespoons vegetable oil
½ cup popcorn
¼ cup melted unsalted polyunsaturated margarine

½ teaspoon Morton Lite Salt mixture

Place oil in a heavy 4-quart saucepan or deep-fryer. Add 1 kernel popcorn and place over medium high heat. When kernel pops, remove it and add remaining popcorn. Stir to mix popcorn and oil. Place cover on pan, leaving a small air space at the edge of the cover to let steam escape. Shake pan frequently until popping stops. Near the end of the popping, remove cover completely and stir until the last few kernels pop. Remove from heat. Add margarine and salt and toss well. Turn into a warm bowl and serve immediately. Makes about 3 quarts.

Per Recipe

Calories	1118	Sodium	558 mg.
Carbohydrate	61 Gm.	Potassium	740 mg.
Protein	10 Gm.	Cholesterol	0
Fat	95 Gm.		

QUICK GAZPACHO

1 cup water
1 lb. fresh tomatoes, peeled and diced
1 cucumber, peeled and sliced
¼ cup mixed vegetable flakes
1 tablespoon onion powder
¼ teaspoon garlic powder
¼ teaspoon Morton Lite Salt mixture

⅛ teaspoon ground red pepper
¼ cup olive or vegetable oil
2 tablespoons wine vinegar

* * *

Croutons, diced tomato and cucumber (optional)

In jar of electric blender, combine all ingredients except oil and vinegar. Cover and blend until almost smooth. Stir in oil and vinegar. Chill well. Serve in bowls and, if desired, garnish with croutons, diced tomato and cucumber. Serves 4.

Per Serving

Calories	215	Sodium	89 mg.
Carbohydrate	21 Gm.	Potassium	368 mg.
Protein	3 Gm.	Cholesterol	0
Fat	14 Gm.		

POTATO SOUP

2 tablespoons unsalted polyunsaturated margarine
1 large onion, finely chopped
5 large potatoes, peeled and cut in small pieces

1 cup water
3 cups milk
2 teaspoons Morton Lite Salt mixture
Pepper to taste

Heat margarine in large saucepan. Add onion and cook until tender. Add potatoes and water; bring to boil and boil gently for 15 minutes, or until potatoes are tender. Mash the mixture. Gradually stir in milk and seasonings. Heat slowly to serving temperature, stirring occasionally to prevent sticking. Makes 6 cups.

Per Cup Serving

Calories	186	Sodium	432 mg.
Carbohydrate	21 Gm.	Potassium	988 mg.
Protein	6 Gm.	Cholesterol	13 mg.
Fat	8 Gm.		

BEEF-VEGETABLE SOUP

1 lb. beef short ribs
7 cups water
2 teaspoons Morton Lite Salt mixture
⅛ teaspoon pepper
2 cups tomatoes, peeled and diced (fresh or canned)

1 cup diced potatoes
¾ cup thin-sliced carrots
½ cup sliced onions
3 cups other mixed vegetables (peas, cabbage, celery, green beans, green pepper, corn)

The day before you plan to serve this soup combine beef, water and salt in a large saucepan. Bring to a boil; cover and simmer until meat can be easily removed from bones. Remove meat to cutting board. Discard bones and visible fat. Return to broth and chill overnight. Next day, lift off and discard fat layer. Reheat, adding remaining ingredients; cover and cook for 35 minutes, or until all vegetables are tender. (If any of the vegetables are canned or cooked, add them during the last 5 minutes of cooking time.) Taste and adjust seasoning. Makes 10 cups.

Per Cup Serving

Calories	99	Sodium	244 mg.
Carbohydrate	9 Gm.	Potassium	440 mg.
Protein	5 Gm.	Cholesterol	15 mg.
Fat	5 Gm.		

BEEF NOODLE SOUP

1¼ lbs. beef short ribs
1 tablespoon Morton Lite Salt mixture
6 cups water

1 cup celery with leaves, chopped
4 oz. uncooked noodles

The day before you are planning to serve this soup, place beef, salt, and water in a large saucepan. Bring to a boil, reduce heat, and simmer, covered, about 2 hours, or until meat is tender. Remove beef to cutting board. Discard bones and visible fat. Cut meat into small pieces. Return meat to broth and refrigerate. Next day, lift off and discard fat layer. Reheat soup to boiling. Add celery; cover and simmer for 10 minutes. Stir in noodles. Cover and simmer about 10 minutes, or until noodles are tender. Makes 6 cups.

Per Cup Serving

Calories	197	Sodium	588 mg.
Carbohydrate	14 Gm.	Potassium	861 mg.
Protein	10 Gm.	Cholesterol	89 mg.
Fat	11 Gm.		

BEAN CHOWDER

¾ cup dry navy beans
4 cups water
1½ teaspoons Morton Lite Salt mixture
¾ cup diced potato
½ cup chopped onion

1½ teaspoons flour
1 tablespoon unsalted polyunsaturated margarine
¾ cup canned tomatoes
⅓ cup minced green pepper
1½ cups milk

The day before, wash and pick over beans. Place in saucepan with water, bring to a boil, cook for 2 minutes, remove from heat and let stand, covered, overnight. Next day, add salt and bring to a boil. Cover and boil until almost done (about 1 hour). Add potato and onion; cook for 30 minutes more. Combine flour with margarine and stir in. Add tomatoes and green pepper. Cook over low heat for 10 minutes, stirring constantly until thickened, then occasionally to prevent scorching. Stir in milk and heat to serving temperature. Makes 4½ cups.

Calories	248	Sodium	478 mg.
Carbohydrate	36 Gm.	Potassium	1027 mg.
Protein	13 Gm.	Cholesterol	9 mg.
Fat	6 Gm.		

NEW ENGLAND FISH CHOWDER

½ cup onion flakes
3⅓ cups water
2 tablespoons vegetable oil
2 cups sliced potatoes
¼ cup mixed vegetable flakes
2 teaspoons Morton Lite Salt mixture
½ teaspoon garlic powder
¼ teaspoon ground black pepper

2 cups milk
2 tablespoons flour
2 small bay leaves
2 lbs. frozen fish fillets, thawed and cut in chunks

* * *

1½ teaspoons parsley flakes
½ teaspoon paprika

Let onion flakes stand in ⅓ cup of the water for 10 minutes. In a large saucepan, heat oil. Add onion and sauté for 5 minutes. Remove from heat. Add remaining 3 cups of water, potatoes, vegetable flakes, salt, garlic powder and black pepper. Bring to a boil. Reduce heat; cover and simmer for 15 minutes, or until potatoes are almost tender. Combine milk and flour. Slowly stir into saucepan; add bay leaves and fish. Simmer, without boiling, for 15 minutes, or just until fish flakes easily with a fork. Remove bay leaves. Ladle into bowls, sprinkling each serving with parsley and paprika. Makes 10 cups.

Per Cup Serving

Calories	405	Sodium	363 mg.
Carbohydrate	67 Gm.	Potassium	501 mg.
Protein	25 Gm.	Cholesterol	68 mg.
Fat	5 Gm.		

BROTH FROM LEFTOVERS

When you have beef roast left over from a company meal, don't discard the rack. Put the bones, along with the meat clinging to them, into a soup kettle and add about a quart of water and, if you like, a peeled onion and a few celery tops. Bring to a boil, reduce heat and simmer gently for 2 hours. Turn the pieces of meat-and-bones from time to time. Strain the resulting broth into a bowl and refrigerate. Next day, lift off and discard the fat layer. The broth will probably have some sediment at the bottom which can be used for flavoring gravies. The rest may be used for beef broth.

Making excellent turkey broth is an easy task. After you have removed most of the meat from the carcass, break it into pieces and put it into the soup kettle. You may also add all the skin and any meaty pieces your family does not plan to eat. Onion and celery may be added for flavor. Simmer for 2 to 3 hours, turning bones occasionally. Remove bones, taking off any salvageable meat. Strain the broth into a bowl. Chill. The next day remove the fat layer. The broth may be frozen or used within 3 days. A good quick soup may be had by bringing broth to a boil, adding any reserved meat and fine noodles or rice. Taste, and add Morton Lite Salt mixture and pepper as needed. The carcass of a 20-pound turkey will make about 1½ quarts of flavorful broth.

Even if your family enjoys eating chicken breasts and legs only, it is always cheaper to buy whole chickens cut up. Use the parts you like for frying or broiling; make a soup from the remainder. Place necks, wing tips, backs and giblets in a saucepan and cover with water. Season as desired. Simmer for 2 hours. Strain the broth, chill, remove fat and use broth as desired within 3 days, or freeze for a longer period.

(See also Simmered Chicken, page 72.)

CHICKEN AND MUSHROOM BROTH

1 quart homemade chicken
  broth
½ teaspoon Morton Lite Salt
  mixture
1 carrot, thinly sliced

¼ lb. fresh mushrooms
¼ lb. spinach, washed and
  chopped
1 tomato, peeled and diced

In a medium saucepan, combine broth, salt and carrot.
Bring to a boil. Reduce heat, cover and simmer for 5 to 8
minutes. Rinse mushrooms and pat dry. Trim off stem
ends and slice. Add to broth along with spinach and
tomato. Cover and simmer for 5 minutes. Makes 6 cups.

Per Cup Serving

Calories	30	Sodium	168 mg.
Carbohydrate	3 Gm.	Potassium	359 mg.
Protein	3 Gm.	Cholesterol	0
Fat	1 Gm.		

CHICKEN GUMBO

4 cups homemade chicken
  broth
½ cup canned or cooked tomatoes
½ cup thin sliced green pepper
½ cup thin sliced onion
1 teaspoon Morton Lite Salt
  mixture

1 tablespoon minced parsley
2 cups cooked, diced chicken
1 package (10 oz.) frozen
  okra, cut up
½ cup cooked rice
½ cup cooked corn

Heat chicken broth, adding tomatoes, green pepper, onion, salt and parsley. Bring to a boil, reduce heat and simmer about 20 minutes, or until onion and pepper are tender. Add chicken and okra; cook 5 minutes longer. Add
rice and corn and heat through. Makes 2 quarts.

Per Cup Serving

Calories	106	Sodium	199 mg.
Carbohydrates	12 Gm.	Potassium	414 mg.
Protein	10 Gm.	Cholesterol	24 mg.
Fat	3 Gm.		

HOMEMADE BEEF BROTH

3 lbs. soup bones
1 lb. beef stew meat, cut up (optional)
3 quarts water
1 tablespoon Morton Lite Salt mixture
⅓ cup celery, chopped

⅓ cup carrots, diced
⅓ cup onion, chopped
2 sprigs parsley, chopped
5 whole cloves
1 bay leaf
Other seasonings as desired

If you buy your meat at a supermarket, the butcher may need advance notice to provide you with soup bones, which should be sawed into pieces to expose more marrow. You may also use bones cut from a roast—even leftover bones. Cut off all the meat from the bones before cooking. A good stock may be made using nothing except beef stew meat, although this is more expensive. Oil the bottom of a stew pot or Dutch oven, add meat and brown well. (This step insures a rich brown color for the stock.) Then cover bones and browned meat with water. Add salt and remaining ingredients. Cover and simmer for 3½ to 4 hours. (In place of some of the water, you can use vegetable liquids from cooking.) Taste the stock and adjust seasonings. At this point, if you have used stew meat, the meat should be removed for use in croquettes, hash, etc. Strain the remaining broth into a bowl. Refrigerate overnight. Next day, lift off and discard the fat layer. Use broth as desired. It should be heated to boiling at least every other day to prevent spoilage, or used within 3 days, or frozen. Makes 2 quarts.

Per Cup Serving

Calories	54	Sodium	345 mg.
Carbohydrate	1 Gm.	Potassium	624 mg.
Protein	2 Gm.	Cholesterol	6 mg.
Fat	4 Gm.		

Beef Soup: After straining the broth you can save all the cooked vegetables and meat and, after overnight storage to remove fat, heat these foods in some of the broth for a fine soup. It may be seasoned with thyme, garlic, nutmeg, cloves, sage, poultry seasoning, Tabasco sauce or cayenne.
Bouillon: To clarify the broth to make bouillon, follow

this procedure. To each quart of cold stock add the beaten white and crushed shell of 1 egg. Bring slowly to a boil, stirring constantly. Boil about 5 minutes. Add ½ cup of cold water and let stand for 10 minutes. Strain through cheesecloth.

Note: Nutrients will vary with cut of beef and the care in skimming off fat.

FRENCH ONION SOUP

5 cups thin sliced sweet Spanish onions
¼ cup unsalted polyunsaturated margarine
3 tablespoons flour
2 quarts homemade chicken or beef broth

Morton Lite Salt mixture to taste
¼ teaspoon white pepper

* * *

Cognac (optional)

Onions may be sliced to form rings or the circles may be cut into quarters for easier eating. In a heavy saucepan or Dutch oven, melt margarine. Add onions and toss lightly until coated with margarine. Reduce heat, cover and cook until wilted and tender (10 to 15 minutes). For a dark onion soup, allow onions to brown a little. Remove cover. Add flour and stir to mix well. Cook for 3 minutes over low heat. Add broth. (Beef broth is traditional, but chicken broth produces a soup with an unusually delicious flavor.) Taste, and add salt as desired. Add pepper. Reduce heat to simmer and cover; cook gently for 1 hour to develop flavor. Makes 2 quarts.

To Freeze: The cooled soup may be placed in appropriate containers and frozen. The soup should be thawed in the refrigerator for a full day, then reheated very slowly. A little cognac (¼ cup for half the recipe) may be added just before serving.

Per Cup Serving

Calories	135	Sodium	139 mg.
Carbohydrate	14 Gm.	Potassium	44 mg.
Protein	6 Gm.	Cholesterol	3 mg.
Fat	7 Gm.		

DILLED CUCUMBER SLICES

2 cucumbers
½ teaspoon Morton Lite Salt mixture
⅛ teaspoon coarse ground black pepper

2 teaspoons snipped fresh dill or 1 teaspoon dill weed
¼ cup vinegar

Wash and peel cucumbers and cut into very thin slices. Arrange in a bowl, sprinkling each layer with salt, pepper and dill. Pour vinegar over all. Cover and chill at least 2 hours. Serve with pierced spoon, or drain well. Slices may be used to top hamburgers in the buns in place of pickles. Makes 6 or more servings.

Per Serving

Calories	7	Sodium	94 mg.
Carbohydrate	2 Gm.	Potassium	141 mg.
Protein	trace	Cholesterol	0
Fat	trace		

ONION AND RED PEPPER RELISH

1 lb. sweet Spanish onions
1½ lbs. sweet red peppers
Boiling water
1 cup cider vinegar

½ cup sugar
2½ teaspoons Morton Lite Salt mixture

Peel onions and cut into small sections to make about 1 quart. Remove seeds, stems and any green spots from red peppers and cut into strips. Grind onions and peppers, using coarse blade of food chopper. Cover with boiling water and let stand 5 minutes. Drain in strainer. Combine onion and pepper with remaining ingredients in saucepan. Bring to a boil and simmer for 20 minutes. Cool, then store covered in the refrigerator. Makes about 3 cups.

Per Recipe

Calories	776	Sodium	2911 mg.
Carbohydrate	193 Gm.	Potassium	3640 mg.
Protein	17 Gm.	Cholesterol	0
Fat	2 Gm.		

PATIO CORN RELISH

1½ teaspoons dry mustard
1½ teaspoons warm water
4 ears corn, uncooked
1½ cups water
¾ cup cider vinegar
⅓ cup sugar
1¼ teaspoons Morton Lite
Salt mixture

½ teaspoon celery seed
½ teaspoon ground turmeric
2 cups shredded cabbage
½ cup onion flakes
¼ cup sweet pepper flakes
¼ cup diced pimiento

Combine mustard with water and let stand for 10 minutes to develop flavor. Meanwhile, cut kernels from corn to make about 2¾ cups. Set aside. In a medium saucepan, combine mustard with 1½ cups of water, vinegar, sugar, salt, celery seed and turmeric. Bring to boil. Add cabbage, onion and sweet pepper flakes plus the reserved corn. Reduce heat to simmer. Cook, covered, for 25 minutes, stirring occasionally. Stir in pimiento and cook 5 minutes longer. May be spooned into hot sterile jars and sealed immediately, or stored in the refrigerator. Makes 2½ pints.

Per Recipe

Calories	931	Sodium	1558 mg.
Carbohydrate	217 Gm.	Potassium	4434 mg.
Protein	21 Gm.	Cholesterol	0 mg.
Fat	6 Gm.		

SPICED BROILED ORANGE BOATS

2 medium-size oranges
½ teaspoon cinnamon

½ teaspoon mace

Cut oranges in half crosswise. Remove seeds and, with small sharp knife, loosen sections. Sprinkle each half with a little of the cinnamon and mace. Broil for 7 minutes, or until hot and lightly browned. Serve with meat, fish, or poultry as appetizer-relish. Serves 4.

Per Serving

Calories	36	Sodium	1 mg.
Carbohydrate	9 Gm.	Potassium	100 mg.
Protein	trace	Cholesterol	0
Fat	trace		

CURRIED FRUIT APPETIZER

¼ cup chopped onion
1 clove garlic, minced
½ teaspoon Morton Lite Salt mixture
2½ teaspoons curry powder
½ teaspoon ginger
½ teaspoon dry mustard
¼ teaspoon pepper

2 tablespoons vinegar
1 tablespoon lemon juice
2 teaspoons honey
¼ cup tomato juice
2 apples, cored and cut in cubes
2 pears, cored and cut in cubes
1½ cups halved, seeded grapes
6 bananas

In a large saucepan, mix onion, garlic, salt, spices, vinegar, lemon juice, honey and tomato juice. Place over low heat, cover and simmer for 15 minutes. Cool. In a large bowl, combine apples, pears and grapes. Just before serving, slice bananas and mix in, then toss with curry dressing and serve. Makes 6 servings.

Per Serving

Calories	238	Sodium	121 mg.
Carbohydrate	57 Gm.	Potassium	156 mg.
Protein	3 Gm.	Cholesterol	0
Fat	1 Gm.		

CHILI PEAR BROIL

3 pears
2 tablespoons unsalted polyunsaturated margarine
2 tablespoons honey
Dash nutmeg

½ teaspoon chili powder
¼ teaspoon Morton Lite Salt mixture
Dash pepper

Cut pears in half and remove cores. Arrange, cut side up, on broiling rack. Mix remaining ingredients and brush over pears. Set broiling rack so pears are about 6 inches from heat. Broil for 10 to 12 minutes, brushing with sauce occasionally. Serve with meat. Serves 6.

Per Serving

Calories	118	Sodium	49 mg.
Carbohydrate	21 Gm.	Potassium	188 mg.
Protein	trace	Cholesterol	0
Fat	4 Gm.		

SESAME PEARS

3 ripe pears
Lemon juice
2 tablespoons sugar
½ cup bread crumbs

2 tablespoons unsalted polyunsaturated margarine, melted
2 teaspoons sesame seeds

Wash the pears. Cut them in half lengthwise and core.
Brush cut surfaces with lemon juice and sprinkle each
with 1 teaspoon of sugar. Broil, cut side up, 6 inches from
heat source, about 8 minutes. Meantime combine bread
crumbs, margarine and sesame seeds. Sprinkle over pears
and broil for 2 to 3 minutes more, or until lightly
browned. Nice with chicken. Serves 6.

Per Serving

Calories	174	Sodium	62 mg.
Carbohydrate	26 Gm.	Potassium	136 mg.
Protein	3 Gm.	Cholesterol	6 mg.
Fat	8 Gm.		

CRANBERRY-ORANGE RELISH

1 lb. (4 cups) cranberries
2 small oranges, quartered and
seeded

1½ cups sugar

Wash and drain cranberries. Put cranberries and oranges
through coarse blade of food chopper. Stir in sugar; chill.
Makes 3 cups.

Note: Mixture may be put into suitable containers and frozen for future use. Allow to thaw in refrigerator for 24
hours before serving.

Per Recipe

Calories	1437	Sodium	11 mg.
Carbohydrate	366 Gm.	Potassium	760 mg.
Protein	4 Gm.	Cholesterol	0
Fat	3 Gm.		

HARVEST RELISH

1 lb. (4 cups) cranberries	2 cups sugar
2 small oranges, quartered and seeded	1 stalk celery, diced
	¼ cup chopped nuts

Wash and drain cranberries. Grind cranberries and oranges, using coarse blade of food chopper. Stir in sugar, celery and chopped nuts. Chill for several hours to blend flavors. Makes 1 quart.

Per Recipe

Calories	2066	Sodium	272 mg.
Carbohydrate	474 Gm.	Potassium	900 mg.
Protein	10 Gm.	Cholesterol	0
Fat	25 Gm.		

CHAPTER 4

MAIN DISHES

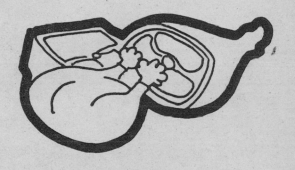

CHAPTER 4

MAIN DISHES

The chief function of main dishes, nutritionally speaking, is to provide protein for the body. Meat, poultry and fish also contain significant amounts of vitamins and minerals, at least one of which (B_{12}) is found only in animal protein.

In recent years we have become aware that meat also contains fat, both saturated and unsaturated.

The leaner cuts of beef—those which do not have a large amount of fat marbled throughout the lean—may be a wiser choice than an elegant filet mignon. Since pork is similar to beef in fattiness, it is best to cook it by dry-heat methods (below). Generally, most of the fat of lamb is easy to trim away. Veal is naturally low in fat. White fish is also lean by nature. Poultry products contain fat, but it is mostly under the skin and is easy to avoid.

If you wish to avoid saturated fat in cooking, choose dry-heat methods—roasting or broiling. Much fat drips away during cooking and, unless you make a gravy with it, is not served. If you stew meat, do it the day before you plan to serve it. Put it in a bowl in the refrigerator overnight; next day, lift off the layer of solid fat which forms on top. Reheat. You'll never miss the calories that were skimmed off!

Poaching or braising also releases fat from meat and poultry, although this fat passes into the cooking liquid.

49

Charcoal cooking is just like other forms of broiling and roasting. It reduces the fat in the meat while it adds a distinctive flavor of its own. This book does not include timetables for charcoal broiling since such times are difficult to predict. The heat of the fire and the amount of wind outdoors enter into how fast the meat cooks.

If you want to charcoal broil, let the coals burn until they are "white hot," covered with a light gray ash. Then put the meat on a grill over them. The broiling times given in this chapter will be the minimum times it takes the meat to be done through. If there is any breeze you will need more time. To test, cut into the meat and judge its pinkness.

A creative cook tries a new main dish at least once a month. (Or perhaps she knows how to make three hundred main dishes so her family is never bored.) The recipes which follow will give you a good running start!

Meat

TARRAGON-BROILED HAMBURGERS

1 lb. ground lean beef
¼ cup fresh lemon juice
¼ cup unsalted polyunsaturated margarine, melted

½ teaspoon tarragon leaves
½ teaspoon Morton Lite Salt mixture

Shape meat into 4 equal patties. Blend remaining ingredients. Brush over both sides of burgers. Broil for 6 to 7 minutes on one side. Turn, baste and broil for 3 minutes, or until meat has browned. Makes 4 patties.

Per Serving

Calories	216	Sodium	180 mg.
Carbohydrate	1 Gm.	Potassium	583 mg.
Protein	26 Gm.	Cholesterol	77 mg.
Fat	12 Gm.		

SLIM-LINE BEEF PATTIES

½ teaspoon dry mustard
1 tablespoon warm water
1 lb. ground lean beef
1 cup finely diced fresh mushrooms
1 cup finely chopped peeled tomato, drained

2 teaspoons instant minced onion
½ teaspoon Morton Lite Salt mixture
¼ teaspoon pepper
⅛ teaspoon garlic powder

Mix mustard with 1 tablespoon of warm water and let stand for 10 minutes to develop flavor. Combine mustard with remaining ingredients; mix well. Shape into 4 patties. Broil for 6 to 7 minutes; turn and brown second side, about 3 minutes. Makes 4 patties.

Per Serving

Calories	160	Sodium	192 mg.
Carbohydrate	4 Gm.	Potassium	820 mg.
Protein	27 Gm.	Cholesterol	77 mg.
Fat	4 Gm.		

OATMEAL MEAT LOAF NEAPOLITAN

2 lbs. ground lean beef
1 cup quick-cooking oatmeal
1 can (8 oz.) tomato sauce
½ cup chopped onion
½ cup chopped green pepper
2 lightly beaten eggs

1½ teaspoons Morton Lite Salt mixture
¼ teaspoon crushed rosemary
¼ teaspoon crushed oregano
¼ teaspoon crushed basil

In a large bowl, mix all ingredients well. Pack into 9″ ×5″ ×3″ loaf pan, handling gently. Bake at 400° for 1 hour, 15 minutes or until top is browned. Drain fat. Let stand in pan for 5 minutes; slice. Makes 8 servings.

Per Serving

Calories	221	Sodium	391 mg.
Carbohydrate	11 Gm.	Potassium	816 mg.
Protein	30 Gm.	Cholesterol	145 mg.
Fat	6 Gm.		

SAVORY MEAT LOAF

1 egg, lightly beaten
¾ teaspoon Morton Lite Salt mixture
⅛ teaspoon pepper
¾ cup cooked or canned tomatoes, cut up, with liquid
¾ cup soft bread cubes
¼ cup finely chopped celery with leaves
¼ cup minced parsley
⅓ cup finely chopped onion
1½ lbs. lean ground beef
¼ lb. bulk pork sausage

In a large bowl, blend ingredients together in order given. Pack into 9″ × 5″ × 3″ loaf pan. Bake at 350° for 1½ hours. Drain fat. Let stand for 5 minutes; slice. Makes 8 slices.

For a Meat Loaf with Crusty Sides: Choose a shallow baking pan (13″ × 9″ × 2″, for example). Press, knead and pat meat into a long narrow loaf shape. Bake as above. Use two pancake turners to lift onto platter.

Per Slice

Calories	202	Sodium	172 mg.
Carbohydrate	4 Gm.	Potassium	686 mg.
Protein	23 Gm.	Cholesterol	102 mg.
Fat	10 Gm.		

BEEF AND RICE SKILLET DINNER

2 tablespoons vegetable oil
1 lb. lean stewing beef, cut in 1-inch cubes
3 cups water
1 can (6 oz.) tomato paste
1 cup uncooked rice (not precooked variety)
1 medium onion, cut in half slices
1 large tomato, peeled and cut in half slices
1½ teaspoons Morton Lite Salt mixture
¾ teaspoon crushed red pepper

Heat oil in large skillet over medium heat. Add beef; brown on all sides, turning as needed. Add 1 cup of water. Cover and simmer for 45 minutes, or until meat is tender. Add remaining 2 cups of water; gradually stir in tomato paste. Add rice, onion, tomato, salt and pepper.

Bring to boil. Cover; reduce heat and simmer, stirring occasionally, for 25 minutes, or until rice is tender. Makes 5 servings.

Per Serving

Calories	425	Sodium	405 mg.
Carbohydrate	31 Gm.	Potassium	859 mg.
Protein	33 Gm.	Cholesterol	59 mg.
Fat	18 Gm.		

ONION TOPPED BEEF BAKE

1 medium sweet Spanish onion	½ teaspoon thyme
1 tablespoon vegetable oil	1 green pepper, cleaned and
2 lbs. lean ground beef	diced
2 teaspoons Morton Lite Salt	3 medium potatoes
mixture	1 can (15 oz.) tomato sauce
½ teaspoon pepper	Parsley, for garnish

Peel and thinly slice onion. Sauté in vegetable oil until just tender. Remove to absorbent paper. Brown ground beef slowly in skillet; drain. Blend in salt, pepper and thyme. Add green pepper. Peel and thinly slice potatoes. Place half of potato slices on bottom of 2½-quart buttered casserole. Top with half the ground beef mixture. Repeat layers. Top with onion rings. Pour tomato sauce over all. Cover and bake at 350° for 1 hour and 15 minutes, or until potatoes and onions are tender. Serve garnished with parsley. Makes 6 servings.

Per Serving

Calories	291	Sodium	761 mg.
Carbohydrate	19 Gm.	Potassium	1356 mg.
Protein	38 Gm.	Cholesterol	103 mg.
Fat	7 Gm.		

STIFADO (Greek Beef Stew)

3 tablespoons vegetable oil
2½ lbs. lean boneless beef stew
   meat, cut in 2-inch cubes
½ cup onion flakes
2¼ cups water
3 tablespoons flour
1 can (6 oz.) tomato paste
¼ cup cider vinegar

1 stick (4-inch) cinnamon,
   broken in half, or ¾
   teaspoon ground cinnamon
4 whole cloves
2 teaspoons Morton Lite Salt
   mixture
½ teaspoon pepper

In Dutch oven or large heavy saucepan, heat oil. Add beef and brown well on all sides. Meantime, let onion flakes stand in ¼ cup of water for 10 minutes. Add to meat and cook for 3 minutes. Stir in flour; cook 2 minutes longer. Pour in remaining 2 cups of water along with remaining ingredients. Bring to boil. Cover; reduce heat and simmer for 1½ hours, or until meat is tender. Remove cinnamon stick and cloves before serving. Makes 6 servings.

Per Serving

Calories	327	Sodium	420 mg.
Carbohydrate	12 Gm.	Potassium	1250 mg.
Protein	38 Gm.	Cholesterol	78 mg.
Fat	12 Gm.		

BEEF CARBONNADE

½ cup onion flakes
⅓ cup water
2½ lbs. lean boneless beef stew
   meat, cut in 2-inch cubes
⅓ cup flour
¼ cup vegetable oil
1 can (12 oz.) beer

2 teaspoons Morton Lite Salt
   mixture
¼ teaspoon garlic powder
¼ teaspoon ground nutmeg
¼ teaspoon powdered thyme
¼ teaspoon pepper

Mix onion flakes and water and let stand for 10 minutes. Place beef in plastic bag with flour and shake to coat beef well. In a Dutch oven or large heavy skillet, heat oil. Add beef and brown on all sides. Add onion; sauté for 5 minutes. Stir in remaining ingredients. Cover; reduce heat and simmer for 1½ hours, or until meat is tender. Makes 6 servings.

Per Serving

Calories	357	Sodium	410 mg.
Carbohydrate	10 Gm.	Potassium	950 mg.
Protein	37 Gm.	Cholesterol	78 mg.
Fat	14 Gm.		

HUNGARIAN GOULASH

1 cup onion flakes	¼ teaspoon powdered
⅔ cup water	marjoram
3 tablespoons vegetable oil	2½ cups water
2½ lbs. lean boneless beef stew	¾ cup dry white wine
meat, cut in 1½-inch cubes	¼ cup sweet pepper flakes
2 tablespoons paprika	¼ cup flour
1¾ teaspoons Morton Lite Salt	⅓ cup water
mixture	* * *
¼ teaspoon pepper	Poppyseed Noodles
	(page 171), (optional)

Mix onion flakes with ⅔ cup of water and let stand for 10 minutes. In a large Dutch oven or heavy skillet, heat 2 tablespoons of oil. Add onion; sauté for 5 minutes. Remove onion; set aside. Add remaining oil to pan. Add meat; brown well on all sides. Sprinkle with paprika, salt, pepper and marjoram. Stir in 2½ cups of water, wine, pepper flakes and sautéed onion. Bring to boil. Reduce heat; cover and simmer for 2 hours, or until meat is tender. Remove to serving platter. Strain gravy into saucepan. Mix flour with remaining ⅓ cup of water. Gradually blend into gravy. Cook, stirring constantly, until thickened. Spoon over beef cubes. If desired, serve with Poppyseed Noodles (page 171). Makes 8 servings.

Per Serving

Calories	258	Sodium	275 mg.
Carbohydrate	8 Gm.	Potassium	675 mg.
Protein	28 Gm.	Cholesterol	58 mg.
Fat	9 Gm.		

OLD-FASHIONED POT ROAST

1 lean brisket of beef (3½ lbs.)
2 tablespoons vegetable oil
1 cup cooked or canned tomatoes
1 cup water
1 teaspoon Morton Lite Salt mixture
1 small bay leaf
2 teaspoons onion powder
½ teaspoon coarse-ground black pepper
¼ teaspoon instant minced garlic

Brown meat in oil in large Dutch oven or heavy saucepan, turning so all sides are crusty. Add remaining ingredients. Cover* and simmer for 3 to 3¼ hours, or until tender, turning meat occasionally. Pour gravy into small bowl and place in freezer until fat forms hard layer across top. (Meantime, keep meat warm.) Discard fat layer. Return gravy to pan and heat until boiling. Makes 8 servings.

*Option: Bake, covered, at 325° for 3 to 3½ hours, or until tender.

Per Serving

Calories	196	Sodium	209 mg.
Carbohydrate	1 Gm.	Potassium	1050 mg.
Protein	24 Gm.	Cholesterol	70 mg.
Fat	10 Gm.		

ROAST VEAL

For a roast veal, buy leg, loin, rib (rack) or rolled shoulder. Place seasoned meat, fat side up, on a rack in an open pan. Bake at 300° to 325°. (A meat thermometer placed in the largest muscle will register 170° when veal is well done.) The following timetable will help.

Cut	Roasting Time
Leg, 5 to 8 lbs.	25–35 minutes per lb.
Loin, 4 to 6 lbs.	30–35 minutes per lb.
Rib (rack), 3 to 5 lbs.	35–40 minutes per lb.
Rolled shoulder, 4 to 6 lbs.	40–45 minutes per lb.

Per 4-oz. Serving

Calories	86	Sodium	62 mg.
Carbohydrate	0	Potassium	75 mg.
Protein	14 Gm.	Cholesterol	69 mg.
Fat	3 Gm.		

VEAL WITH LEMON

1½ lbs. veal round steak, boned and cut ¼ inch thick
½ teaspoon Morton Lite Salt mixture
Pepper
¼ cup flour
¼ cup vegetable oil
1 cup homemade chicken broth

½ teaspoon tarragon, crushed
1 teaspoon grated lemon peel
1 teaspoon fresh lemon juice
2 to 4 tablespoons water

* * *

Lemon Cartwheels
Minced parsley

Cut veal into serving pieces. Score edges to prevent curling. Season with salt and pepper and coat with flour. Heat oil in large skillet. Add veal pieces, a few at a time, and cook until browned on both sides. Remove from pan. Drain off all but 1 tablespoon of pan drippings. Add broth, tarragon, lemon peel and juice. Bring to a boil, scraping drippings loose from bottom of pan. Add browned cutlets; simmer very gently for 5 minutes or until tender. Remove to warm serving platter. Add water to drippings, using just enough to make sauce thin but not watery. Add Lemon Cartwheels (see below) and heat just a few seconds. Remove and top each serving with 1 or 2 Lemon Cartwheels; cover with sauce. Sprinkle generously with snipped parsley and serve. Makes 6 servings.

Lemon Cartwheels: Use 1 large or 2 small lemons. Cut away outer yellow peel, then peel again, leaving a thin but intact layer of white membrane. (Without membrane, slices will fall apart.) Slice lemons paper thin, less than ⅛ inch. You will need 2 pretty slices for each piece of veal.

Per Serving

Calories	169	Sodium	261 mg.
Carbohydrate	4 Gm.	Potassium	417 mg.
Protein	15 Gm.	Cholesterol	72 mg.
Fat	10 Gm.		

ITALIAN VEAL CHOPS

½ cup vegetable oil
3 medium onions, sliced (4 cups)
6 veal chops, cut ½ inch thick
⅓ cup flour
½ cup water

2 tablespoons lemon juice
2 tablespoons chopped parsley
2 teaspoons Morton Lite Salt mixture
½ teaspoon oregano

Heat oil in large skillet over medium heat. Add onion; sauté about 5 minutes, or until slightly tender. Remove from skillet. Dredge veal chops with flour. Brown, turning once. Add onions with remaining ingredients. Cover and simmer for 25 to 30 minutes, or until meat is tender. Makes 6 servings.

Per Serving

Calories	365	Sodium	415 mg.
Carbohydrate	17 Gm.	Potassium	930 mg.
Protein	22 Gm.	Cholesterol	41 mg.
Fat	23 Gm.		

VEAL PAPRIKA

½ cup vegetable oil
3 medium onions, sliced (4 cups)
1 clove garlic, minced
2 lbs. veal shoulder, cut in 1-inch cubes
2 cups water
½ green pepper, cut in strips

3 tablespoons paprika
2 tablespoons chopped parsley
2 teaspoons Morton Lite Salt mixture
3 tablespoons cornstarch
* * *
Hot cooked noodles

Heat oil in large Dutch oven or kettle. Add onion and garlic; sauté until onion is tender. Remove. Add veal; brown on all sides, turning as needed. Add onion, 2 cups of water, green pepper, paprika, parsley and salt. Cover and simmer gently for 1 hour, or until tender. Mix together cornstarch and 2 tablespoons of water until smooth. Stir into veal mixture. Bring to boil, stirring constantly, and boil for 1 minute. Serve with hot noodles. Makes 6 servings.

Calories	314	Sodium	421 mg.
Carbohydrate	8 Gm.	Potassium	813 mg.
Protein	20 Gm.	Cholesterol	90 mg.
Fat	22 Gm.		

APPLE-STUFFED VEAL ROLLS

8 tablespoons (1 stick) unsalted polyunsaturated
margarine
½ cup chopped onion
3 cups day-old white bread
cubes
1 cup diced apple

½ teaspoon Morton Lite Salt
mixture
Generous dash pepper
1½ cups apple juice
1 lb. thin veal cutlets

* * *

Chopped parsley

Melt 6 tablespoons of the margarine in a large skillet. Add onion. Sauté, stirring occasionally, until golden, about 5 minutes. Stir in bread cubes. Heat, stirring, until margarine is absorbed. Stir in apple, salt, pepper and ¼ cup of the apple juice; set aside. Place each veal cutlet between sheets of waxed paper. Pound very thin with smooth-surfaced meat hammer or rolling pin; do not tear meat. Remove waxed paper. Top cutlets with apple mixture. Roll up as for jelly roll. Fasten with toothpicks or tie with string. Melt remaining 2 tablespoons of margarine in skillet. Add veal rolls. Brown on all sides over medium heat. Add remaining 1¼ cups of apple juice and any remaining stuffing. Cover; reduce heat and simmer for 30 to 35 minutes, or until veal is fork-tender and liquid is reduced to a thick glaze. To serve, spoon glaze over veal, then sprinkle with chopped parsley. Makes 4 servings.

Per Serving

Calories	568	Sodium	175 mg.
Carbohydrate	38 Gm.	Potassium	667 mg.
Protein	21 Gm.	Cholesterol	42 mg.
Fat	38 Gm.		

VEAL À LA MODE

1½ lbs. veal shoulder, cut in 2-inch cubes
1½ lbs. tomatoes, peeled and diced
1 small bay leaf
½ teaspoon powdered thyme
¼ teaspoon garlic powder

1 teaspoon Morton Lite Salt mixture
Dash pepper
4 small potatoes, peeled and cubed
1 package (10 oz.) frozen cut green beans

Spread veal cubes in a shallow baking pan. Brown on all sides under a hot broiler. Transfer meat with juices to a medium-size heavy saucepan. Add tomatoes and seasonings. Cover and simmer over low heat for 1 hour, or until meat is almost tender. Add potatoes and cook 15 minutes more. Add beans and continue cooking 15 minutes more. Makes 6 servings.

Per Serving

Calories	266	Sodium	220 mg.
Carbohydrate	19 Gm.	Potassium	827 mg.
Protein	21 Gm.	Cholesterol	42 mg.
Fat	12 Gm.		

ROAST LAMB

For roast lamb, buy a leg, a half leg, a rolled shoulder, a cushion shoulder or a rib cut. Season meat (use Morton Lite Salt mixture and pepper, and rub with a cut clove of garlic if desired) and place, fat side up, on a rack in an open pan. Bake at 300° to 325°. A meat thermometer inserted in the largest muscle will register 155° to 160° for rare, 165° to 170° for medium or 175° to 180° for well done. Use the following timetable as a rough guide:

	Approximate Cooking Time (Minutes per lb.)		
Cut	Rare	Medium	Well Done
Leg, 4 to 8 lbs.	25–27	28–30	32–34
Shoulder, 4 to 6 lbs.	25–27	28–30	30–35
Rolled, 3 to 5 lbs.	25–27	28–30	35–45
Cushion, 3 to 5 lbs.	25–27	28–30	30–35
Rib, 1½ to 3 lbs.*	25–27	28–31	35–45

*Roast rib at 375°.

Calories	96	Sodium	41 mg.
Carbohydrate	0	Potassium	210 mg.
Protein	14 Gm.	Cholesterol	49 mg.
Fat	4 Gm.		

BROILED LAMB

The cuts of lamb that can be broiled are shoulder chops, rib chops, loin chops and ground lamb patties. Grease the broiling rack before placing lamb on it. Preheat the broiler if needed. If lamb is ¾ to 1 inch thick, set rack so top surface of meat is 2 to 3 inches from source of heat. Place it 3 to 5 inches away if cut is 1 to 2 inches thick. Broil until top side is brown, season with Morton Lite Salt mixture and pepper, then turn and brown other side. Season again and serve. Use the timetable below as a rough guide:

	Total Approximate Cooking Time, Minutes		
Cut	*Thickness*	*Rare*	*Medium*
Shoulder chops	1 inch	6–7	12
	1½ inches	9–10	18
Rib chops	1 inch	6–7	12
	1½ inches	9–10	18
	2 inches	12–14	22
Loin chops	1 inch	6–7	12
	1½ inches	8–9	18
	2 inches	9–10	22
Ground lamb patties	1 inch	10–12	18

Broiled 1½-inch rib chop

Calories	119	Sodium	54 mg.
Carbohydrate	0	Potassium	384 mg.
Protein	10 Gm.	Cholesterol	57 mg.
Fat	8 Gm.		

LAMB, GREEK STYLE

1 5-lb. leg of lamb
1 tablespoon Morton Lite
   Salt mixture
2 teaspoons crushed oregano
¼ teaspoon pepper

½ cup flour
2 cloves garlic, crushed
1 teaspoon grated lemon peel
⅓ cup lemon juice
¼ to ⅓ cup water

With point of sharp knife, make slashes about 2 inches apart over entire surface of roast, cutting about ½ inch deep and ¾ inch long. Thoroughly combine seasonings, flour, garlic and lemon peel. Add only enough lemon juice to form a smooth not too thick paste. Rub over entire roast, working it into each opening with fingers.

Place on rack in shallow roasting pan. Bake at 350° for 1¾ hours. If meat thermometer is available, insert it now and continue baking until dial registers 180°, for 40 to 45 minutes more. Carefully lift out lamb to carving board or platter and let stand for 10 to 15 minutes. Meanwhile transfer drippings into small saucepan; skim off fat. Blend in water; heat and serve with lamb. Makes 8 servings.

Per Serving

Calories	269	Sodium	515 mg.
Carbohydrate	6 Gm.	Potassium	925 mg.
Protein	35 Gm.	Cholesterol	122 mg.
Fat	10 Gm.		

SHISH KABOB

Marinade:

⅔ cup vegetable oil
⅓ cup wine vinegar
1 tablespoon Morton Lite Salt
   mixture
½ teaspoon crushed rosemary

¼ teaspoon coarse-ground
   black pepper
1 bay leaf
1 clove garlic, minced

Kabobs:

1 lb. boneless lamb, cut in 1½-
   inch cubes
6 to 8 small white onions, par-
   boiled

½ lb. large mushroom caps
1 tomato, cut in wedges
1 medium green pepper, cut in
   2-inch pieces

Combine ingredients for marinade in shallow dish. Prick lamb cubes; add, with vegetables, to marinade. Cover and refrigerate for at least 3 hours, or overnight, turning frequently. Arrange marinated meat and vegetables separately on metal skewers. (Vegetables will cook more quickly than the meat.) Broil 3 inches from heat, turning occasionally, about 15 minutes or until tender. Makes 4 servings.

Per Serving

Calories	244	Sodium	324 mg.
Carbohydrate	5 Gm.	Potassium	816 mg.
Protein	15 Gm.	Cholesterol	49 mg.
Fat	18 Gm.		

ARMENIAN GROUND LAMB KABOBS

½ cup instant minced onion
¾ cup water
2 tablespoons unsalted polyunsaturated margarine
2 lbs. lean ground lamb
1 lightly beaten egg

2 tablespoons parsley flakes
1¾ teaspoons Morton Lite Salt mixture
¾ teaspoon ground cumin
⅛ teaspoon coarse-ground black pepper
12 cherry tomatoes

Mix onion and water and let stand for 10 minutes. In small skillet, melt margarine. Add half the onion and cook gently for 4 minutes. In a large mixing bowl, combine the sautéed onion with lamb, egg, parsley flakes, salt, cumin and black pepper. Mix well. Shape into small oblongs about 2 inches long and ¾ inch in diameter. Arrange meat and tomatoes on separate skewers. (Tomatoes will cook more quickly than meat.) Broil 3 inches from heat for 10 to 12 minutes, or until done to taste, turning often. Makes 6 servings.

Per Serving

Calories	192	Sodium	390 mg.
Carbohydrate	3 Gm.	Potassium	718 mg.
Protein	20 Gm.	Cholesterol	111 mg.
Fat	10 Gm.		

LAMB STEW

⅓ cup flour
1½ teaspoons Morton Lite Salt mixture
⅛ teaspoon pepper
1½ lbs. boneless stew lamb, cut in 1-inch cubes
2 tablespoons oil

3¼ cups water
3 medium onions, sliced
4 medium potatoes, cut into 1-inch cubes
5 medium carrots, quartered
1½ cups fresh peas

Combine flour, salt and pepper; coat lamb cubes thoroughly with mixture. Heat oil in Dutch oven or deep kettle. Add lamb and brown on all sides. Empty remaining seasoned flour out of bag over lamb; stir. Add water; cover tightly. Simmer 1½ to 2 hours, or until lamb is tender. Add onions, potatoes and carrots; simmer, covered, for 15 minutes. Add peas. Simmer, covered, until vegetables are all tender, stirring occasionally. Makes 6 servings.

Per Serving

Calories	258	Sodium	322 mg.
Carbohydrate	25 Gm.	Potassium	925 mg.
Protein	18 Gm.	Cholesterol	49 mg.
Fat	9 Gm.		

LAMB CURRY

3 tablespoons flour
1 teaspoon Morton Lite Salt mixture
1½ lbs. boneless stew lamb, cut in 1-inch cubes
2 tablespoons unsalted polyunsaturated margarine
1 medium-size onion, sliced

1 medium-size tart apple, diced
1 tablespoon curry powder
¾ cup orange juice
* * *
Rice (optional)
Garnish: Pineapple cubes, chopped peanuts or pecans (optional)

Blend flour and salt; coat lamb cubes thoroughly with mixture. Heat margarine in skillet. Add lamb and brown on all sides. Add onion, apple and curry powder; cook for 2 to 4 minutes, or until onion is tender. Add orange juice and simmer, covered, until lamb is tender, about 1 hour.

Check liquid occasionally. If mixture seems dry, add a bit of water. Good with rice; may be garnished with heated canned pineapple cubes and chopped peanuts or pecans. Makes 4 servings.

Per Serving

Calories	274	Sodium	341 mg.
Carbohydrate	17 Gm.	Potassium	844 mg.
Protein	22 Gm.	Cholesterol	73 mg.
Fat	13 Gm.		

ROAST PORK

All the cuts in the chart below may be roasted. Preheat the oven to 325°. Place the roast on a rack, fat side up. Season with Morton Lite Salt mixture and pepper and, if desired, rub with grated lemon peel. A meat thermometer in the largest muscle will register 170° when pork is well done. Use the timetable below to help in planning:

Cut		Weight		Cooking Time (Minutes per lb.)
Loin	Center	3–5	lbs.	30–35
	Half	5–7	lbs.	35–40
	Rolled	3–5	lbs.	35–45
Picnic shoulder		5–8	lbs.	30–35
	Rolled	3–5	lbs.	35–40
Fresh ham, whole, bone in		12–16	lbs.	22–26
	whole, rolled	10–14	lbs.	24–28
	half, bone in	5–8	lbs.	35–40

Per 4-oz. Serving

Calories	116	Sodium	34 mg.
Carbohydrate	0	Potassium	190 mg.
Protein	12 Gm.	Cholesterol	44 mg.
Fat	7 Gm.		

BROILED PORK CHOPS

Have rib or loin pork chops cut ¾ to 1 inch thick. Place on rack of broiling pan. Preheat broiler if needed. Place pan in broiler so top of meat is 2 to 3 inches from source of heat. Broil until top side is brown, about 12 minutes. Season with Morton Lite Salt mixture and pepper. Turn and cook for 8 to 12 minutes more.

Per Broiled Pork Chop (¾ inch)

Calories	314	Sodium	184 mg.
Carbohydrate	0	Potassium	500 mg.
Protein	26 Gm.	Cholesterol	76 mg.
Fat	23 Gm.		

APPLE-STUFFED PORK CHOPS

¼ cup instant minced onion	1½ teaspoons Morton Lite Salt mixture
½ cup water	⅛ teaspoon ground pepper
1 tablespoon unsalted polyunsaturated margarine	1 lightly beaten egg
1¾ cups toasted small bread cubes	6 rib pork chops, 1 inch thick, with pocket
½ cup diced peeled apple	1 tablespoon vegetable oil
¾ teaspoon poultry seasoning	1½ cups orange juice

Mix onion with ¼ cup of the water; let stand 10 minutes. In a small skillet, melt margarine, add onion, and cook gently for 5 minutes. In a mixing bowl, blend onion with bread cubes, apple, poultry seasoning, ½ teaspoon of the salt, pepper, egg and the remaining ¼ cup of water. Spoon about 2 tablespoons of this stuffing into the pocket of each pork chop. Fasten with toothpicks. Sprinkle with remaining salt and add pepper to taste. Heat the oil in a heavy skillet. Add pork chops and brown on both sides. If skillet is ovenproof, use as casserole; otherwise, transfer chops into shallow baking dish. Pour orange juice over all. Cover and bake at 375° for 1 hour, or until tender. Makes 6 servings.

Calories	641	Sodium	343 mg.
Carbohydrate	16 Gm.	Potassium	1075 mg.
Protein	30 Gm.	Cholesterol	153 mg.
Fat	50 Gm.		

PORK CHOPS JARDINIÈRE

1 tablespoon vegetable oil
4 loin pork chops
½ cup chopped onion
1 tablespoon flour
1 cup chopped, peeled tomatoes
½ cup orange juice
½ cup water
1½ teaspoons Morton Lite Salt mixture
½ teaspoon crushed thyme
1 avocado, peeled and sliced
2 oranges, peeled and sliced

Heat oil in skillet. Add pork chops and brown on both sides. Remove. Add onion to skillet and cook until tender. Sprinkle with flour; stir to mix well. Add tomatoes, orange juice, water, salt and thyme. Add pork chops, turn to coat. Cover and simmer for 1 hour, or until meat is tender, turning once. Add sliced avocado and oranges; heat through. Makes 4 servings.

Per Serving

Calories	507	Sodium	472 mg.
Carbohydrate	22 Gm.	Potassium	1300 mg.
Protein	29 Gm.	Cholesterol	76 mg.
Fat	35 Gm.		

OLD-FASHIONED STUFFED CABBAGE

1 head (3 lbs.) green cabbage
1 lb. ground lean pork
½ lb. ground lean beef
1½ cups cooked rice
2 tablespoons parsley flakes
1½ teaspoons Morton Lite
  Salt mixture
1 teaspoon onion powder

¼ teaspoon ground red pepper
1 can (1 lb.) tomatoes, broken
  up
1 can (8 oz.) tomato sauce
1 teaspoon dill seed
½ teaspoon sugar
Dash pepper

Core the cabbage. Place it in a large kettle containing boiling water to cover. Cook until leaves separate from head, removing them as this occurs. Drain leaves. Trim thick center vein from cabbage leaves, being careful not to tear leaves. Set leaves aside.

In a mixing bowl, combine pork, beef, rice, parsley flakes, 1¼ teaspoons of salt, onion powder and red pepper. Mix well. Place a heaping tablespoon of filling in the center of each leaf. Fold 2 sides over filling; roll up. In a Dutch oven or large skillet, place leftover cabbage. Lay stuffed cabbage on top, seam side up. Combine tomatoes, tomato sauce, dill seed, sugar, ¼ teaspoon salt and pepper; mix well. Pour over stuffed cabbage. Cover; bring to boiling point. Reduce heat and simmer 2 to 2½ hours. Makes 10 portions, or 26 cabbage rolls.

Per Serving

Calories	177	Sodium	361 mg.
Carbohydrate	18 Gm.	Potassium	62 mg.
Protein	13 Gm.	Cholesterol	30 mg.
Fat	6 Gm.		

ENROLLADOS

6 medium tomatoes (2 lbs.), diced
2 cups shredded cooked pork*
½ cup chopped onion
1 clove garlic, minced
1½ cups diced cooked potatoes
2 tablespoons unsalted polyunsaturated margarine
1¾ teaspoons Morton Lite Salt mixture
½ teaspoon pepper
½ teaspoon crushed red pepper
12 tortillas
1 small head lettuce, shredded
½ cup fresh onion rings
1 tablespoon vegetable oil
¼ teaspoon ground oregano

Purée tomatoes in blender. Strain and set aside. In large skillet, cook pork, onion, garlic, potatoes and ⅓ of the puréed tomatoes in margarine for 10 minutes. Add 1¼ teaspoons of salt, ¼ teaspoon of pepper and red pepper. Heat tortillas as directed on package. Spoon 2 tablespoons of this mixture on each. Roll up and arrange on shredded lettuce. Sauté onion rings in oil in skillet. Add remaining tomato purée, salt, pepper and oregano. Mix well. Cook for 5 minutes. Spoon over Enrollados. Makes 6 servings.

*Option: Shredded chicken or turkey may be substituted.

Per Serving

Calories	252	Sodium	334 mg.
Carbohydrate	42 Gm.	Potassium	1016 mg.
Protein	6 Gm.	Cholesterol	88 mg.
Fat	8 Gm.		

Poultry

Most of us are eating more poultry today than we did twenty years ago. Both chicken and turkey are relatively inexpensive forms of protein. They, and their somewhat more expensive cousin, the rock Cornish hen, are also fairly low in saturated fat.

Following are some recipes, both basics and more complex ones, to keep your family happily eating poultry once or twice a week. A word of caution: Duck and goose are higher in fat and should be avoided from a calorie standpoint.

ROAST CHICKEN

Buy whole chickens as large as possible. Wash inside and out with cold water, drain, then sprinkle neck and body cavities with 1 teaspoon of Morton Lite Salt mixture per chicken. If desired, stuff. Hook wing tip onto back to hold neck skin; tie legs together, then to tail. Place chicken directly in shallow pan; a rack is unnecessary. If desired, brush chicken with vegetable oil. Roast according to timetable. If chicken is stuffed, increase total roasting time by 15 minutes. To test for doneness, drumstick meat should feel soft when pressed between fingers and leg should twist easily out of thigh joint. If bird is 2 pounds or less, roast at 400°. Chickens over 2 pounds should be roasted at 375°.

Weight	Time (per lb.)	Approx. Amount Stuffing	Approx. Total Time
1½ lbs.	40 min.	¾ cup	1 hr.
2 lbs.	35 min.	1 cup	1 hr. 10 min.
2½ lbs.	30 min.	1¼ cups	1 hr. 15 min.
3 lbs.	30 min.	1½ cups	1 hr. 30 min.
3½ lbs.	30 min.	1¾ cups	1 hr. 45 min.
4 lbs.	30 min.	2 cups	2 hrs.
4½ lbs.	30 min.	2¼ cups	2 hrs. 15 min.
5 lbs.	30 min.	2½ cups	2 hrs. 30 min.

Per 6-oz. Serving

Calories	256	Sodium	642 mg.
Carbohydrate	26 Gm.	Potassium	662 mg.
Protein	22 Gm.	Cholesterol	67 mg.
Fat	7 Gm.		

RICE STUFFING FOR CHICKEN

¾ cup uncooked long-grain rice
⅓ cup unsalted polyunsaturated margarine
½ cup chopped onion

½ cup chopped green pepper
½ teaspoon sage
¼ teaspoon thyme
⅛ teaspoon pepper

Cook rice according to package directions, using Morton Lite Salt mixture. Melt margarine in skillet. Add chopped onion and green pepper; cook, stirring occasionally, until tender. Add cooked rice, sage, thyme and pepper. Toss lightly with fork. Use to stuff chicken. Enough for one 4-pound bird. Serves 5.

Per Recipe

Calories	209	Sodium	8 mg.
Carbohydrate	18 Gm.	Potassium	68 mg.
Protein	2 Gm.	Cholesterol	0
Fat	15 Gm.		

FOIL-ROASTED CHICKEN WITH VEGETABLES

1 whole broiler-fryer chicken (2½ to 3 lbs.)
Morton Lite Salt mixture
Pepper
Paprika
4 carrots, pared and sliced

1 lb. green beans, cut into pieces, or 1 package (10 oz.) frozen cut green beans
2 large potatoes, peeled and cut into quarters

* * *

Chopped parsley

Sprinkle chicken cavity with salt and pepper. Hook wing tip onto back to hold neck skin; tie legs together. Place chicken across center of a 24-inch piece of heavy-duty aluminum foil. Sprinkle with paprika. Arrange vegetables around chicken. Sprinkle with more salt and pepper. Bring ends of foil together over chicken; make a double fold and another double fold at each end. Place in a shallow roasting pan. Bake at 450° for 1 hour. Open foil and fold back; roast for 20 minutes longer. Sprinkle with chopped parsley and remove to serving platter. Serves 4.

Per Serving

Calories	314	Sodium	267 mg.
Carbohydrate	14 Gm.	Potassium	1400 mg.
Protein	37 Gm.	Cholesterol	109 mg.
Fat	11 Gm.		

LEMON-BROILED CHICKEN

¼ cup lemon juice
1 teaspoon grated lemon peel
1 teaspoon vegetable oil
½ teaspoon Morton Lite Salt mixture
½ teaspoon ground ginger

½ teaspoon paprika
¼ teaspoon onion powder
¼ teaspoon pepper
1 broiler-fryer chicken, 2½ lbs., quartered

In a small bowl, combine all ingredients except chicken; mix well. Brush over chicken. Place on broiling pan, skin side down. Broil 9 inches from heat source for 20 minutes. Turn. Continue broiling, turning and basting occasionally until browned and crisp, for 25 minutes, or until done. Makes 4 servings.

Per Serving

Calories	233	Sodium	189 mg.
Protein	2 Gm.	Potassium	1000 mg.
Carbohydrate	30 Gm.	Cholesterol	91 mg.
Fat	11 Gm.		

SIMMERED CHICKEN

1 broiler-fryer chicken, whole or cut in serving pieces
2 cups water
1 small onion, sliced

3 celery tops
1 teaspoon Morton Lite Salt mixture
¼ teaspoon pepper

Put chicken in a large pot; add water and remaining ingredients. Bring to a boil; cover tightly. Reduce heat and simmer for 1 hour, or until tender, adding extra water as needed. Remove from heat; strain broth and, if desired, store in a covered jar in the refrigerator. When chicken is cool, remove meat from skin and cut into chunks for use in salads or other dishes. One broiler-fryer yields about 2½ cups of cut-up cooked chicken and 2 to 2½ cups broth. Serves 5.

Per Serving

Calories	215	Sodium	225 mg.
Carbohydrate	2 Gm.	Potassium	736 mg.
Protein	27 Gm.	Cholesterol	80 mg.
Fat	10 Gm.		

PEAR CHICKEN BAKE

1 can (1 lb. 13 oz.) Bartlett pear halves
1 can (8 oz.) crushed pineapple
1 can (6 oz.) frozen pineapple-grapefruit concentrate
1 teaspoon Morton Lite Salt mixture
¼ teaspoon curry powder
¼ teaspoon ginger
½ cup unsalted polyunsaturated margarine
1 broiler-fryer chicken, 3 to 4 lbs., cut up
2 teaspoons cornstarch

Drain pears, reserving syrup. Drain pineapple and measure ½ cup of fruit. Set aside. Pour remaining pineapple and pineapple syrup into saucepan. Add juice concentrate, ½ cup of pear syrup, seasonings and margarine. Heat to boiling. Place chicken parts in shallow baking pan and baste with hot fruit mixture. Bake at 375° for 1 hour, or until tender, basting frequently. Fill pear halves with reserved pineapple; brush with basting sauce and broil until lightly browned, or bake at 375° for 10 minutes. Pour basting sauce into saucepan. Add a little to cornstarch and return to remaining basting sauce. Cook, stirring constantly, until thickened. Serve hot pear halves and sauce with chicken. Makes 6 servings.

Per Serving

Calories	398	Sodium	228 mg.
Carbohydrate	21 Gm.	Potassium	869 mg.
Protein	24 Gm.	Cholesterol	72 mg.
Fat	23 Gm.		

HERB-BAKED CHICKEN WITH WINE SAUCE

¼ cup unsalted polyunsaturated margarine, softened
1 teaspoon Morton Lite Salt mixture
⅛ teaspoon pepper
⅛ teaspoon rosemary
⅛ teaspoon thyme

Generous dash garlic powder
Generous dash onion powder
4 chicken breasts (about 1½ lbs.)
1 cup water
2 tablespoons flour
2 tablespoons dry white wine

Combine margarine and seasonings. Arrange chicken breasts, skin side down, in large baking dish. Spread half the margarine mixture on chicken. Bake at 400° for 30 minutes. Turn chicken; spread with remaining margarine mixture. Bake for 30 minutes longer, or until done. Remove chicken to serving platter; keep warm. Gradually blend water into flour. Stir into drippings. Heat, stirring, until thickened. Add wine; heat. Serve sauce over chicken. Makes 4 servings.

Per Serving

Calories	248	Sodium	368 mg.
Carbohydrate	4 Gm.	Potassium	150 mg.
Protein	24 Gm.	Cholesterol	81 mg.
Fat	13 Gm.		

OVEN-FRIED CHICKEN

1 broiler-fryer chicken, 2½ to 3 lbs., cut up
½ cup fine dry bread crumbs or flour

2 teaspoons Morton Lite Salt mixture
1 teaspoon paprika
¼ teaspoon pepper
¼ cup vegetable oil

Wash chicken and pat dry. Mix together bread crumbs or flour with salt, paprika and pepper. Coat chicken with this mixture. Pour oil in shallow baking pan. Arrange chicken pieces in pan, skin side down. Bake at 400° for 30 minutes. Turn chicken and continue baking about 30 minutes, or until tender. Makes 4 servings.

Calories	417	Sodium	691 mg.
Carbohydrate	8 Gm.	Potassium	1433 mg.
Protein	37 Gm.	Cholesterol	113 mg.
Fat	25 Gm.		

CHICKEN WITH PEACHES

1 broiler-fryer, 2½ to 3½ lbs., cut up and skinned
½ teaspoon Morton Lite Salt mixture
½ cup flour
1 can (1 lb. 13 oz.) peach halves or slices
¼ cup unsalted polyunsaturated margarine
¼ cup orange juice
½ cup walnuts

Wash chicken and pat dry. Sprinkle with salt and coat with flour, shaking off excess. Place in medium shallow baking dish. Drain peaches, saving ¾ cup of syrup. Melt margarine in small saucepan; stir in orange juice and peach syrup. Pour over chicken. Bake at 375°, basting several times with juices in dish, for 1 hour. Add peaches and walnuts and continue baking, basting once, for 15 minutes, or until chicken is tender and glazed. Makes 4 servings.

Per Serving

Calories	575	Sodium	202 mg.
Carbohydrate	35 Gm.	Potassium	1100 mg.
Protein	39 Gm.	Cholesterol	109 mg.
Fat	31 Gm.		

BAKED CHICKEN WITH GRAPES

1 broiler-fryer chicken, about 2½ lbs., cut up
1 cup water
2 tablespoons finely chopped onion
1 teaspoon Morton Lite Salt mixture
¾ teaspoon thyme
¼ teaspoon pepper
⅛ teaspoon minced garlic
4 teaspoons cornstarch
4 teaspoons water
1 cup seedless green grapes
1 tablespoon cooking sherry

Wash chicken and pat dry. Place in shallow baking dish, about 15″ × 10″. Add water. Combine onion, salt, thyme, pepper and garlic; sprinkle over chicken. Bake, uncovered, at 350° for 1½ hours, or until tender. Remove chicken to serving dish. Drain drippings into saucepan. Add cornstarch mixed with water and stir over medium heat until thickened. Add grapes and sherry and heat through. Pass this sauce with the chicken. Makes 4 servings.

Per Serving

Calories	234	Sodium	328 mg.
Carbohydrate	4 Gm.	Potassium	1031 mg.
Protein	30 Gm.	Cholesterol	91 mg.
Fat	9 Gm.		

CHICKEN CACCIATORE

1 broiler-fryer, 2½ to 3½ lbs., cut up
¼ cup flour
¼ cup vegetable oil
1 medium onion, chopped
1 medium green pepper, chopped
1 clove garlic, minced
1¼ teaspoons Morton Lite Salt mixture
⅛ teaspoon pepper
2 bay leaves
1 can (1 lb.) whole tomatoes, cut up
1 can (8 oz.) tomato sauce
* * *
2 tablespoons chopped parsley

Wash chicken and pat dry. Coat with flour. Heat oil in large skillet. Add chicken and cook over medium heat, turning as needed, until lightly browned on all sides. Remove from skillet. Add onion, green pepper and garlic to oil and cook about 3 minutes. Add chicken; spoon sautéed vegetables over chicken. Add salt, pepper, bay leaves, tomatoes and tomato sauce. Cover and simmer for 25 minutes, or until chicken is tender. Remove bay leaves. Serve garnished with parsley. Makes 4 servings.

Per Serving

Calories	514	Sodium	608 mg.
Carbohydrate	19 Gm.	Potassium	1287 mg.
Protein	40 Gm.	Cholesterol	109 mg.
Fat	31 Gm.		

CHICKEN SCALLOPINE

8 chicken thighs, boned*	2 tablespoons chopped parsley
1 teaspoon Morton Lite Salt mixture	1 tablespoon chopped chives
	¼ teaspoon marjoram
2 tablespoons unsalted polyunsaturated margarine	* * *
1 tablespoon lemon juice	Buttered toast points or rice
	Lemon slices (optional)

Place boned thighs between two pieces of waxed paper. Pound with side of cleaver or rolling pin to flatten. Sprinkle with salt. Melt margarine over medium heat in large skillet. Add chicken, skin side down. Cook about 10 minutes, or until lightly browned. Turn; sprinkle with lemon juice and herbs. Cook about 10 minutes more, until tender. Serve on buttered toast points or rice. If desired, garnish with thin lemon slices. Makes 4 servings.

*To bone chicken thighs: Make a lengthwise cut along thinner side of a broiler-fryer thigh. Scrape flesh away from bone and remove bone.

Per Serving

Calories	185	Sodium	363 mg.
Carbohydrate	4 Gm.	Potassium	1005 mg.
Protein	21 Gm.	Cholesterol	78 mg.
Fat	17 Gm.		

CHICKEN PICCATA

1½ lbs. boned, skinned chicken breasts (3 breasts)
¼ cup unsalted polyunsaturated margarine
1 tablespoon flour
1 teaspoon Morton Lite Salt mixture
1 teaspoon tarragon

½ cup homemade chicken broth
3 thin lemon slices, halved
* * *
Rice (optional)
1 teaspoon finely chopped parsley

Cut chicken breasts into narrow strips. Have all other ingredients ready, and make this dish when the remaining parts of the meal are nearly done. Melt margarine in a large skillet over high heat. Add chicken; sprinkle with flour, salt and tarragon. Cook for 5 minutes, stirring constantly. Add chicken broth and lemon slices; stir to loosen any browned particles. Cover and cook for 2 to 3 minutes. Serve over rice, if desired, or as an appetizer. Sprinkle with chopped parsley. Makes 3 servings.

Per Serving

Calories	278	Sodium	122 mg.
Carbohydrate	2 Gm.	Potassium	700 mg.
Protein	24 Gm.	Cholesterol	87 mg.
Fat	18 Gm.		

POLYNESIAN CHICKEN

2 broiler-fryer chickens, 2½ to 3 lbs. each, cut up
2 teaspoons Morton Lite Salt mixture
1 tablespoon paprika
¼ teaspoon pepper
Vegetable oil
1 can (13½ oz.) pineapple chunks
½ cup orange juice

2 tablespoons lemon juice
¼ cup dark corn syrup
¼ teaspoon mace
⅛ teaspoon ground ginger
1 tablespoon flour
2 tablespoons water
2 oranges, peeled and sliced
* * *
Rice (optional)

Sprinkle chicken with mixture of salt, paprika and pepper. Heat oil in large skillet; brown chicken on all sides. Drain off excess fat. Drain pineapple, saving ½ cup of syrup.

Combine this syrup with orange and lemon juice, corn syrup, mace and ginger. Pour over chicken in skillet. Cover and simmer for 30 minutes, or until tender. Remove chicken to warm serving platter. Mix flour and water together until smooth; slowly stir into sauce in pan; boil for 2 to 3 minutes. Add drained pineapple and orange slices; heat just until warm. Pour over chicken and serve at once. Serve with rice if desired. Makes 8 servings.

Per Serving

Calories	360	Sodium	337 mg.
Carbohydrate	16 Gm.	Potassium	841 mg.
Protein	36 Gm.	Cholesterol	109 mg.
Fat	16 Gm.		

CRANBERRY-ALMOND CHICKEN

1 broiler-fryer chicken, about 3 lbs., cut up
1 teaspoon Morton Lite Salt mixture
¼ teaspoon pepper
1 teaspoon paprika
⅓ cup unsalted polyunsaturated margarine
1 cup cranberry juice cocktail
½ cup slivered almonds, toasted

Wash chicken and pat dry. Combine salt, pepper and paprika; rub into chicken. Melt margarine in large skillet. Add chicken and brown on all sides. Cover frying pan, reduce heat, and cook for 25 to 30 minutes, or until chicken is tender. Remove to warm platter and keep hot in warm oven. Pour cranberry cocktail into frying pan; stir to loosen all browned particles. Cook over high heat until only ½ cup remains. Pour over chicken. Sprinkle with toasted almonds and serve at once. Makes 4 servings.

Per Serving

Calories	532	Sodium	338 mg.
Carbohydrate	15 Gm.	Potassium	1147 mg.
Protein	40 Gm.	Cholesterol	108 mg.
Fat	36 Gm.		

MOO GOO GAI PAN

1 lb. boned and skinned chicken breasts (2 breasts)
½ teaspoon Morton Lite Salt mixture
⅛ teaspoon pepper
2 tablespoons vegetable oil
2 tablespoons sliced green onions
1 cup sliced fresh mushrooms
2 tablespoons sliced pimiento

¼ teaspoon ground ginger
1 cup homemade chicken broth
1 package (about 7 oz.) frozen snow peas, thawed enough to separate
1 tablespoon cornstarch
2 tablespoons water
* * *
Hot cooked rice

Cut chicken into 1-inch cubes. Sprinkle with salt and pepper. Heat oil in skillet over medium heat. Add chicken; cook, stirring constantly, until chicken turns white throughout. Remove from skillet. Add green onions and cook 1 minute; stir in mushrooms, pimiento and ginger; cook for 3 to 5 minutes, or until mushrooms are tender. Add broth and snow peas. Bring to boil, separating snow peas with fork. Mix cornstarch and water until smooth; stir into vegetable mixture. Bring to boil, stirring constantly, and boil for 1 minute. Return chicken to skillet. Reduce heat to low; cook for 2 to 3 minutes, or until chicken is hot. Serve with rice. Makes 4 servings.

Per Serving

Calories	177	Sodium	232 mg.
Carbohydrate	11 Gm.	Potassium	522 mg.
Protein	15 Gm.	Cholesterol	39 mg.
Fat	8 Gm.		

JELLIED ORANGE CHICKEN SALAD

2 envelopes unflavored gelatin
¼ cup sugar
¼ teaspoon Morton Lite Salt mixture
2 cups water
1 can (6 oz.) frozen orange juice concentrate, undiluted
½ cup tarragon vinegar

4 oranges, peeled and sectioned
1 cup diced cooked chicken or 1 can (6 oz.) chicken, diced
½ cup minced celery
* * *
Lettuce leaves

Mix gelatin, sugar and salt in saucepan. Stir in 1 cup of the water. Place over low heat, stirring constantly, until gelatin and sugar are dissolved (about 3 to 5 minutes). Stir in remaining cup of water, undiluted orange concentrate and tarragon vinegar. Mix well. Chill until mixture is slightly thicker than unbeaten egg whites. Meanwhile, cut enough orange sections in half to make ½ cup; fold into gelatin mixture with chicken and celery. Turn into 1½-quart mold. Chill until firm. Unmold; garnish with greens and remaining orange sections. If desired, serve with mayonnaise thinned with orange juice. Makes 6 servings.

Per Serving

Calories	219	Sodium	47 mg.
Carbohydrate	35 Gm.	Potassium	577 mg.
Protein	14 Gm.	Cholesterol	20 mg.
Fat	4 Gm.		

CHICKEN SALAD WITH RICE AND AVOCADOS

4 teaspoons lemon juice
1½ cups diced avocado
1 cup cooked, diced chicken
1½ cups cooked rice
½ cup finely chopped celery
1 tablespoon finely chopped green onion

2 tablespoons mayonnaise
2 tablespoons sour cream
1 teaspoon Morton Lite Salt mixture

* * *

Lettuce leaves

Toss lemon juice lightly with avocado. Combine remaining ingredients, except lettuce, and mix well. Add avocado and toss lightly. Chill thoroughly. Serve on crisp lettuce, as a side dish at buffets or a light luncheon dish with finger sandwiches. Makes 4 servings.

Per Serving

Calories	316	Sodium	562 mg.
Carbohydrate	18 Gm.	Potassium	834 mg.
Protein	17 Gm.	Cholesterol	53 mg.
Fat	19 Gm.		

HERBED CHICKEN LIVERS

1 lb. chicken livers, cut in half
¾ teaspoon Morton Lite Salt mixture
⅛ teaspoon pepper
1 tablespoon chopped onion
1 tablespoon chopped parsley
½ teaspoon tarragon
Flour
2 tablespoons unsalted polyunsaturated margarine

Sprinkle livers with salt, pepper, onion, parsley and tarragon. Dust lightly with a little flour. Melt margarine in skillet over medium heat. Add livers and cook about 10 minutes, turning occasionally. Makes 4 servings.

Option: If desired, add ½ cup of dry white wine to pan drippings. Increase heat and cook, stirring constantly, until slightly thickened. Pour over chicken livers.

Per Serving

Calories	222	Sodium	207 mg.
Carbohydrate	5 Gm.	Potassium	450 mg.
Protein	25 Gm.	Cholesterol	340 mg.
Fat	11 Gm.		

TURKEY

Since most turkey is available frozen, buy a reputable brand and follow the label directions for thawing and roasting. To stuff the turkey you may use a packaged stuffing mix, following package directions, or try the recipe below:

SESAME SEED STUFFING

½ cup celery flakes
¼ cup instant minced onion
⅔ cup water
1 cup unsalted polyunsaturated margarine
3 quarts toasted bread cubes
1 cup toasted sesame seeds*
⅓ cup parsley flakes
1 tablespoon Morton Lite
  Salt mixture
¾ teaspoon pepper
¾ cup homemade chicken or turkey broth

Mix celery flakes and onion with water and let stand for 10 minutes. Melt margarine in medium skillet. Add celery and onion and cook until golden. In a large bowl, combine remaining ingredients. Add sautéed celery and onion. Use to stuff neck and body cavity of 12- to 15-pound turkey.

To toast sesame seeds: Sprinkle in a large shallow pan. Toast at 350° for 8 to 10 minutes, or until golden.

Per Serving

Calories	452	Sodium	369 mg.
Carbohydrate	31 Gm.	Potassium	480 mg.
Protein	91 Gm.	Cholesterol	12 mg.
Fat	34 Gm.		

COUNTRY GARDEN CORNISH HENS

2 Rock Cornish game hens, 17 to 22 oz. each, dressed and frozen
⅔ cup sliced celery
⅔ cup sliced onion
½ cup sliced carrots
¼ cup vegetable oil
2 teaspoons Morton Lite Salt mixture
¼ to ½ teaspoon pepper
⅓ cup melted unsalted polyunsaturated margarine
⅓ cup sherry

Thaw hens for 2 to 4 hours at room temperature, or for a day in the refrigerator. Remove giblets and save for another use. With kitchen shears or sharp heavy knife, cut hens in half along breastbone and backbone. Wipe pieces with damp paper towel. Grease a shallow casserole or 9-inch baking pan. Mix vegetables. Arrange in pan in four mounds. Brush or rub hen halves with oil, using 1 tablespoon per half hen. Sprinkle each hen half with salt, using ½ teaspoon for each; then sprinkle each with pepper. With cavity side down, put a hen half on each mound of vegetables. Roast at 375° for about 1 hour, or until juice

83

from hens is no longer pink and the meat is tender. Brush or drizzle melted margarine over hens, using a generous tablespoon for each half. Add sherry to pan. Return to oven for 5 to 10 minutes longer. Or broil for 3 minutes, until golden. Serve vegetables and some pan drippings over each hen half. Makes 4 servings.

Per Serving

Calories	399	Sodium	614 mg.
Carbohydrate	8 Gm.	Potassium	1625 mg.
Protein	13 Gm.	Cholesterol	36 mg.
Fat	34 Gm.		

Fish

The world of frozen fish is so interesting it deserves frequent experimentation. Most fish is low in fat, too, making it a wise choice.

In years past, cookbooks called for only a few varieties of fish. Today some of the time-honored favorites are less available and new species with unfamiliar names appear in freezer cases instead. Happily, it's been found that lean, white-fleshed ocean fish are interchangeable in recipes, if you allow for variations in the thickness of fillets. A recipe for sole, for instance, will work well with Greenland turbot.

As you gain experience with these new varieties you will learn that some seasonings enhance certain species, and you can adjust your recipes accordingly. But by and large substitution is safe.

Since you sometimes can't see the frozen fish you buy, it helps to know just what the lean, white-fleshed ocean fish are called. Here is a list:

Alaska pollock   Ocean catfish
Cod   Ocean perch
Croaker   Sea bass (blackfish)
Flounder   Sea trout (weakfish)
Greenland turbot   Snapper
Grouper   Sole
Haddock   Whiting (hake)
Halibut

The above fish are all available as fillets. Some are also available as steaks or simply drawn and dressed. Halibut is most commonly found in steak form.

FISH STEAKS PROVENÇAL

4 small halibut or cod steaks, 1 inch thick (2½ to 3 lbs.)
¼ cup vegetable oil
1 cup finely chopped onion
½ cup chopped green pepper
1 small clove garlic, minced
1 can (1 lb.) whole tomatoes, drained and halved

1 teaspoon Morton Lite Salt mixture
¼ teaspoon pepper
⅛ teaspoon thyme
⅛ teaspoon basil
⅛ teaspoon cayenne (optional)

If necessary, thaw steaks completely. Thoroughly dry with paper towel. Heat oil in large deep skillet over medium high heat. Add fish steaks and brown lightly, turning once, 2 to 3 minutes. Arrange in baking dish about 12" × 7" × 2". Add onion, green pepper and garlic to skillet. Cook gently until tender. Stir in tomatoes, salt, pepper, thyme, basil and cayenne, and cook about 1 minute. Pour tomato mixture over fish steaks. Bake at 400° for about 15 minutes, or just until fish flakes easily with fork. Makes 8 servings.

Per Serving

Calories	257	Sodium	235 mg.
Carbohydrate	5 Gm.	Potassium	720 mg.
Protein	36 Gm.	Cholesterol	118 mg.
Fat	9 Gm.		

HALIBUT STEAK JARDINIÈRE

1 cup sliced celery
1 medium onion, sliced
1 medium green pepper, cut into ¼ inch strips (1 cup)
¼ cup vegetable oil
1 tablespoon lemon juice
½ teaspoon minced onion
1 halibut steak, 1 inch thick (about 1 lb.)
½ teaspoon Morton Lite Salt mixture
Dash pepper
1 medium tomato, peeled and sliced

Line an 8-inch-square baking dish with celery, onion and green pepper. In shallow bowl, stir together oil, lemon juice and minced onion. Sprinkle both sides of steak with salt and pepper. Dip steak in oil mixture, coating all sides. Place over vegetables in baking dish. Pour any remaining oil mixture over fish and vegetables. Arrange tomato slices on fish. Bake at 350° for 40 to 45 minutes, or just until fish flakes easily with a fork. Makes 3 servings.

Per Serving

Calories	357	Sodium	317 mg.
Carbohydrate	9 Gm.	Potassium	902 mg.
Protein	33 Gm.	Cholesterol	106 mg.
Fat	21 Gm.		

BAKED WHOLE FISH IN FOIL

1 clove garlic, minced
1 teaspoon Morton Lite Salt mixture
1 teaspoon oregano
½ teaspoon basil
½ teaspoon thyme
Dash pepper
½ cup vegetable oil
¼ cup chopped onion
1½ teaspoons grated lemon peel
¼ cup lemon juice
1 whole fish (4 to 5 lbs. dressed, with head and back fin removed)

Mix garlic, salt, herbs and pepper. Stir in oil, onion, lemon peel and juice. Tear off a sheet of heavy-duty aluminum foil twice the length of the fish plus 3 inches. Place foil in baking pan with half the piece extending over one end of the pan. Place fish on foil. Pour marinade over fish. Bring extending half of foil over fish and seal three sides with double folds. Refrigerate for 1 hour. Bake at 375° for about 45 minutes, or until fish flakes easily with fork. Makes 6 servings.

Per 6-oz. Serving

Calories	278	Sodium	190 mg.
Carbohydrate	32 Gm.	Potassium	584 mg.
Protein	15 Gm.	Cholesterol	120 mg.
Fat	1 Gm.		

STUFFED AND BAKED FISH BRUNOISE

1 whole fish (striped bass, sea bass, red snapper, lake trout, white fish), 2 to 5 lbs.
¼ cup unsalted polyunsaturated margarine
1 clove garlic, split
½ cup chopped green pepper
½ cup chopped sweet onion
¼ cup chopped celery

2 tomatoes, peeled and chopped
¼ cup chopped parsley
1 teaspoon Morton Lite Salt mixture
¼ teaspoon pepper

* * *

Lemon or lime wedges

Have your fish dealer scale and clean the fish and remove the head. Wipe fish with damp cloth and place on a greased bake-and-serve platter. Heat margarine in skillet. Place garlic pieces on toothpicks, add to margarine and simmer gently for 5 minutes. Remove garlic. Add pepper, onion and celery and cook over moderate heat, stirring occasionally, long enough to soften (about 5 minutes). Add tomatoes, parsley, salt and pepper, and stir over low heat for 1 minute. Fill fish with as much of this stuffing as possible and arrange the rest (including liquid in pan) over and around the fish. Cover. Bake at 425° until fish flakes easily with a fork. Allow about 30 minutes for a 2- or 3-pound fish, 50 minutes for a 5-pound fish. Serve with wedges of lemon or lime. A 3-pound fish will serve 4.

Per 6-oz. Portion

Calories	240	Sodium	211 mg.
Carbohydrate	3 Gm.	Potassium	586 mg.
Protein	33 Gm.	Cholesterol	119 mg.
Fat	10 Gm.		

NEAPOLITAN FISH FILLETS

1½ lbs. fresh or frozen flounder or haddock fillets
1 medium tomato, peeled and chopped
1 tablespoon minced onion
⅛ teaspoon basil
Vegetable oil
Morton Lite Salt mixture
Pepper

If necessary, partially thaw fillets. Preheat broiler pan and rack for 5 minutes. Combine tomato, onion and basil; set aside. Brush both sides of fillets with oil. Sprinkle with salt and pepper. Place small amount of tomato mixture in center of each fillet. Overlap both ends of fillet over tomato; fasten with wooden picks. Arrange on broiler rack. Broil 3 inches from source of heat, turning once and brushing with oil, about 5 minutes on each side or until fish flakes easily with a fork but is still moist. Makes 6 servings.

Per Serving

Calories	125	Sodium	87 mg.
Carbohydrate	1 Gm.	Potassium	383 mg.
Protein	17 Gm.	Cholesterol	56 mg.
Fat	5 Gm.		

BROILED FILLETS WITH SESAME

1 lb. fresh or frozen fish fillets
¼ cup unsalted polyunsaturated margarine, melted
2 tablespoons sesame seeds

Partially thaw fillets, if needed. Pat dry with paper towel. Brush with melted margarine. Place on rack in broiler pan. Sprinkle with sesame. Broil 4 inches from heat source, basting occasionally with melted margarine, 5 to 7 minutes or until fish is tender and flakes easily when tested with fork. Makes 3 servings.

Per Serving

Calories	363	Sodium	102 mg.
Carbohydrate	4 Gm.	Potassium	466 mg.
Protein	26 Gm.	Cholesterol	85 mg.
Fat	28 Gm.		

SOLE AMANDINE WITH TOMATOES

½ cup flour
1½ teaspoons Morton Lite Salt mixture
⅜ teaspoon pepper
1 lb. sole or flounder fillets
5 tablespoons unsalted polyunsaturated margarine

4 cups chopped, peeled tomatoes (3 to 4 large)
½ clove garlic, minced
½ teaspoon tarragon

* * *

¼ cup slivered, toasted, blanched almonds

Mix together flour, 1 teaspoon of the salt and ¼ teaspoon of the pepper, and coat fillets with this mixture. Melt 4 tablespoons of the margarine in a skillet over low heat. Add fillets; fry for 2 to 3 minutes on each side until golden brown. Keep hot. Meantime, in another skillet, melt remaining tablespoon of margarine. Add tomatoes, garlic, the remaining ½ teaspoon of salt, tarragon and the remaining ⅛ teaspoon of pepper. Cover. Cook over low heat for 2 to 3 minutes, or until tomatoes are heated through. Drain. Arrange tomato mixture on shallow platter. Place fillets on top. Garnish with almonds. Makes 4 servings.

Per Serving

Calories	354	Sodium	484 mg.
Carbohydrate	21 Gm.	Potassium	1022 mg.
Protein	22 Gm.	Cholesterol	57 mg.
Fat	22 Gm.		

ITALIAN BROILED FILLETS

1 lb. fish fillets, fresh or frozen
¼ cup unsalted polyunsaturated margarine, softened
1 tablespoon lemon juice
¼ teaspoon Morton Lite Salt mixture

Dash pepper
½ teaspoon crushed, dried mint leaves
½ teaspoon crushed oregano
Paprika

Partially thaw fillets, if necessary. Arrange fish fillets on greased broiler pan. Blend margarine with lemon juice, salt, pepper, mint and oregano. Spread mixture on fish fillets. Broil in preheated broiler 3 inches from source of heat for 3 to 5 minutes, or until fish flakes easily when tested with a fork. Sprinkle with paprika. Makes 4 servings.

Per Serving

Calories	186	Sodium	134 mg.
Carbohydrate	trace	Potassium	487 mg.
Protein	16 Gm.	Cholesterol	56 mg.
Fat	12 Gm.		

SOLE TOMATE

1½ lbs. sole fillets
1 cup coarsely chopped, peeled tomatoes
½ cup white wine
2 tablespoons flour

2 tablespoons unsalted polyunsaturated margarine
½ teaspoon Morton Lite Salt mixture
¼ teaspoon white pepper
2 tablespoons white wine

Partially thaw fillets if necessary. Arrange in skillet and top with ¾ cup of the tomatoes and ½ cup of wine. Poach, covered, over medium heat until fish flakes easily with a fork (10 to 15 minutes). Remove fish to warm platter. Strain liquid into bowl; discard tomatoes. In same skillet or small saucepan, blend flour into melted margarine. Slowly stir liquid from fish into this mixture. Add salt and pepper; stir until sauce is smooth. Bring just to a boil; reduce heat as low as possible. Stir in remaining 2 tablespoons of wine and the remaining ¼ cup of chopped tomatoes. Replace fish in sauce. Bring just to a simmer. Serve at once. Makes 6 servings.

Per Serving

Calories	150	Sodium	157 mg.
Carbohydrate	4 Gm.	Potassium	549 mg.
Protein	17 Gm.	Cholesterol	56 mg.
Fat	4 Gm.		

GRILLED LAKE SUPERIOR WHITEFISH, MAÎTRE D'HOTEL

¼ cup unsalted polyunsaturated margarine, melted
⅛ teaspoon Morton Lite Salt mixture
Dash pepper

1 whitefish (2 lbs.), cleaned, boned and split lengthwise
1 tablespoon finely chopped parsley
1 teaspoon lemon juice

Grease broiling rack with a little melted margarine. Stir salt and pepper into remaining margarine. Brush insides of whitefish with some of this mixture. Place split fish, skin side up, on broiler rack. Brush skin generously with some of the melted margarine. Reserve remainder. Broil fish under preheated broiler 3 to 4 inches from source of heat for about 10 minutes, or until fish flakes easily with a fork. Place on serving platter. Stir chopped parsley and lemon juice into remaining margarine; pour over fish. Makes 3 servings.

Per Serving

Calories	352	Sodium	117 mg.
Carbohydrate	trace	Potassium	850 mg.
Protein	25 Gm.	Cholesterol	93 mg.
Fat	27 Gm.		

SIERRA MOUNTAIN TROUT SAUTÉ

4 to 6 ready-to-cook whole
  trout, fresh or frozen
Morton Lite Salt mixture
Pepper
⅓ cup cornmeal
Vegetable oil
½ cup unsalted polyunsaturated margarine

¼ cup lemon juice
2 tablespoons sauterne or orange juice
¼ cup minced parsley
2 tablespoons chervil

* * *

Lemon wedges

Thaw trout if frozen. Season with salt and pepper and coat on all sides with cornmeal. Fry in ⅛ inch of hot oil for about 7 minutes on each side, or until fish flakes easily with a fork. Transfer to platter; keep warm. In another skillet, melt margarine and heat until bubbling. Add lemon juice and wine. Bring to a boil. Let bubble for 1 minute. Stir in parsley and chervil. Pour over trout; serve garnished with lemon wedges. Makes 6 servings.

Per Serving

Calories	383	Sodium	95 mg.
Carbohydrate	5 Gm.	Potassium	3100 mg.
Protein	12 Gm.	Cholesterol	46 mg.
Fat	35 Gm.		

Main Dish Sauces

The sauces which follow add variety to otherwise everyday foods. Each has several uses.

SWEET AND SOUR DUCK SAUCE

¼ teaspoon dry mustard
¼ teaspoon warm water
2 teaspoons cornstarch
¼ cup cold water
1 jar (10 oz.) peach or apricot
  preserves

1 tablespoon white vinegar
½ teaspoon ground ginger
⅛ teaspoon Morton Lite Salt
  mixture
Pinch ground cloves
Pinch ground red pepper

In a cup, mix mustard with warm water and let stand for 10 minutes to develop flavor. In a small saucepan, blend cornstarch with cold water. Stir in preserves, vinegar, spices and mustard. Mix well. Bring to boiling point. Reduce heat and simmer for 2 minutes, stirring constantly. Use as a glaze for duck, chicken, roast pork or spareribs, or as a sauce for Chinese foods. Makes 1 cup.

Per Recipe

Calories	1071	Sodium	203 mg.
Carbohydrate	273 Gm.	Potassium	320 mg.
Protein	3 Gm.	Cholesterol	0
Fat	3 Gm.		

HOT BARBECUE SAUCE

2 tablespoons instant minced onion
¼ teaspoon instant minced garlic
2 tablespoons water
2 tablespoons vegetable oil
1 cup homemade chicken broth
1 can (8 oz.) tomato sauce
1 can (6 oz.) tomato paste
3 tablespoons vinegar
2 tablespoons dark brown sugar
2 tablespoons parsley flakes
½ teaspoon ground allspice
¼ teaspoon Morton Lite Salt mixture
¼ teaspoon ground red pepper

Mix onion and garlic with water; let stand for 10 minutes. In a medium saucepan, heat oil. Add onion and garlic; cook for 4 minutes, or until golden. Remove from heat. Add remaining ingredients. Simmer, uncovered, for 15 minutes, stirring occasionally. Use as a basting sauce for chicken, pork chops, spareribs or fish. Makes about 2¼ cups.

Per Recipe

Calories	776	Sodium	768 mg.
Carbohydrate	73 Gm.	Potassium	2400 mg.
Protein	10 Gm.	Cholesterol	10 mg.
Fat	52 Gm.		

SWEET CATSUP SAUCE

1 piece (3 inch) stick
  cinnamon
1 teaspoon whole cloves
1 large garlic clove, chopped
1 cup vinegar
1 can (1 lb. 13 oz.) tomato
  purée

⅓ cup sugar
1¼ teaspoons Morton Lite
  Salt mixture
1 teaspoon paprika
Dash cayenne pepper

Tie cinnamon, cloves and garlic into a cheesecloth bag.
Add to vinegar and simmer over low heat for 15 minutes.
Meantime, place tomato purée in deep saucepan. Heat to
boiling, then reduce heat until purée is plopping gently.
Cook for 15 minutes, stirring frequently. Remove spices
from vinegar, pressing out liquid from bag. Turn tomato
purée into reduced spiced vinegar and stir to blend. Add
sugar, salt, paprika and pepper. Continue cooking and
stirring about 12 minutes more. Store covered in refrigerator. Use to top hamburgers, as a flavoring for baked beans
or as a barbecue sauce. Makes 2 cups.

Per Recipe

Calories	434	Sodium	2878 mg.
Carbohydrate	113 Gm.	Potassium	2628 mg.
Protein	6 Gm.	Cholesterol	0
Fat	1 Gm.		

CRANBERRY GLAZE

1 cup cranberry juice cocktail
1 cup whole cranberry sauce
¼ cup honey
½ cup light corn syrup
¼ cup unsalted polyunsaturated margarine

In small saucepan, cook cranberry juice and sauce until sauce melts. Add remaining ingredients. Simmer for 10 minutes. Use as basting sauce for chicken or turkey during last 45 minutes of cooking. Makes about 2 cups.

Per Recipe

Calories	1613	Sodium	9 mg.
Carbohydrate	303 Gm.	Potassium	80 mg.
Protein	trace	Cholesterol	0
Fat	50 Gm.		

HOT MUSTARD SAUCE, DIJON STYLE

¼ cup dry mustard
¼ cup water
¼ cup vegetable oil
2 teaspoons wine
2 tablespoons mayonnaise
2 teaspoons vinegar
2 teaspoons flour
1 teaspoon sugar
½ teaspoon Morton Lite Salt mixture

Combine all ingredients; mix well. Let stand about 10 minutes before using. Store in refrigerator. Good with cold meats. Makes about ¾ cup.

Per Recipe

Calories	596	Sodium	1330 mg.
Carbohydrate	13 Gm.	Potassium	900 mg.
Protein	4 Gm.	Cholesterol	0
Fat	61 Gm.		

CHAPTER 5

THE VEGETABLES YOU COOK

CHAPTER 5

THE VEGETABLES YOU COOK

If you are seeking to improve your eating habits you will soon learn that cooked vegetables are dear friends. Most are low in calories. They contain no saturated fat, and there are many imaginative ways to dress them up without adding butter or cream. Interesting vegetable dishes and a wide variety of vegetables make menus sparkle.

Many of us like our vegetables in their simplest form and the following pages give you some good ways to achieve this. But you will also want to try some of the fancier recipes—for company, or just as an extra surprise for the family.

A Low-Water Way to Cook Frozen Vegetables

If you have a saucepan or a skillet with a tight-fitting lid, try cooking frozen vegetables by the following method to preserve flavor and "season" vegetables without adding margarine.

In saucepan, place 1 tablespoon of vegetable oil. Add a 9- or 10-ounce package of frozen vegetables and 3 tablespoons of water. Sprinkle with Morton Lite Salt mixture and pepper to taste. Cover and place over medium-low heat. After 2 minutes, break up vegetables with a fork. Shake the pan from time to time to prevent sticking. Cook until tender.

Frozen corn cooks in about 11 minutes, Italian green beans in 17 minutes, cut green beans and frozen cauliflower in 13 minutes. If you like, you may add chopped onion, chopped peeled tomato, sliced canned water chestnuts, chopped pimiento or a desired herb.

"Panned" Fresh Vegetables

The preceding method may be followed with certain fresh vegetables, too. Wash the vegetables but do not dry. For a 1-pound quantity of vegetables, follow these timing directions:

Broccoli, cauliflower, Brussels sprouts or cut green beans: 8 to 16 minutes.

Peas and cubed turnips: 23 minutes.

Check vegetables during cooking; sometimes a little more water should be added.

ASPARAGUS

Choose asparagus which is firm and unblemished. You may prefer large stiff stalks or delicate thin ones, but strive for uniform size so cooking time is the same. Hold each stalk in two hands and snap off the white butt end right around the place it starts to turn green; discard the butt, or use in soups. Wash remaining stalks thoroughly in several changes of lukewarm water. Stalks may be set upright in an asparagus cooker or laid flat in a skillet. Add a small amount (about ½ inch) of boiling water and ½ teaspoon of Morton Lite Salt mixture. Cover and cook for 10 to 20 minutes, or until butt ends are tender. One pound serves 3.

Per Serving

Calories	39	Sodium	186 mg.
Carbohydrate	8 Gm.	Potassium	312 mg.
Protein	4 Gm.	Cholesterol	0
Fat	trace		

ASPARAGUS POLONAISE

2 lb. cooked asparagus
¼ lb. unsalted polyunsaturated margarine
⅔ cup freshly made bread crumbs

1 hard-cooked egg
Juice of 1 lemon
2 tablespoons chopped parsley

Just before asparagus is cooked, melt margarine; add bread crumbs and sauté until golden. Sieve egg yolk and white separately. Place drained asparagus on hot platter. Sprinkle with lemon juice, browned crumbs, sieved egg and parsley. Makes 6 servings.

Per Serving

Calories	228	Sodium	87 mg.
Carbohydrate	15 Gm.	Potassium	80 mg.
Protein	6 Gm.	Cholesterol	44 mg.
Fat	17 Gm.		

GREEN BEANS

Select unblemished crisp fresh beans. With fingers, snap off ends and wash. Beans may be cooked this way or broken or cut into pieces 1½ inches long. To cut beans French-style, place on cutting board and cut on deep diagonal, about ½ inch apart, so much of the bean's interior is exposed.

Place the beans in a heavy saucepan with 1 inch of boiling water. Add ½ teaspoon of Morton Lite Salt mixture per pound. Cover and cook for 15 minutes for French-cut beans, about 25 minutes for whole green beans. Drain. Add unsalted polyunsaturated margarine to taste. One pound serves 4.

Per Serving

Calories	36	Sodium	145 mg.
Carbohydrate	8 Gm.	Potassium	238 mg.
Protein	2 Gm.	Cholesterol	0
Fat	trace		

ITALIAN-STYLE GREEN BEANS

1 tablespoon instant minced onion
¼ teaspoon instant minced garlic
2 tablespoons water
2 tablespoons vegetable oil

2 packages (9 oz. each) frozen cut green beans
1 teaspoon basil
1 teaspoon Morton Lite Salt mixture
⅛ teaspoon pepper

Mix minced onion and garlic with 1 tablespoon of water and let stand for 10 minutes. In a large skillet, heat oil. Add onion and garlic; sauté for 5 minutes. Reduce heat; add green beans, basil, salt, pepper and remaining tablespoon of water. Cover and simmer for 5 to 8 minutes. or until beans are crisp-tender, stirring occasionally. Check frequently so beans don't burn. Makes 6 servings.

Per Serving

Calories	63	Sodium	184 mg.
Carbohydrate	5 Gm.	Potassium	303 mg.
Protein	1 Gm.	Cholesterol	0
Fat	5 Gm.		

DILLY BEANS AND CARROTS

½ lb. fresh green beans
4 medium-sized carrots
¾ cup water
1 teaspoon sugar

½ teaspoon Morton Lite Salt mixture
½ teaspoon dill seed

* * *

¼ cup Basic French Dressing (page 139)

Wash, trim and slice green beans. Cut carrots into thin strips 2 to 3 inches long. Combine water, sugar, salt and dill seed in a saucepan; bring to boil. Add carrots and green beans, cover, and simmer for 5 minutes. Boil until both vegetables are tender and liquid is almost evaporated (about 10 minutes). Add dressing and toss. Serve hot, or chill and use in tossed vegetable salad. Makes 6 servings.

Per Serving

Calories	30	Sodium	116 mg.
Carbohydrate	7 Gm.	Potassium	266 mg.
Protein	1 Gm.	Cholesterol	0
Fat	trace		

BROCCOLI

The best broccoli is dark green, sage green or purple green, with short stems, small leaves and compact buds. Avoid broccoli which shows yellowing or open blossoms. Remove the leaves and cut off tough stalk ends. Soak in cold water containing 2 tablespoons of Morton Lite Salt mixture for 30 minutes. Drain and rinse. Peel off the skin from the main stalks, but leave it on the branches. Make crosswise cuts about 2 inches deep in large stalks. Place in saucepan with 2 inches of boiling water and 1 teaspoon of Morton Lite Salt mixture. Without covering, cook for 3 minutes. Cover and cook for 8 to 18 minutes more, or until stalks are tender. Drain. Sprinkle with lemon juice or top with unsalted polyunsaturated margarine. One pound serves 3.

Calories	48	Sodium	389 mg.
Carbohydrate	9 Gm.	Potassium	600 mg.
Protein	5 Gm.	Cholesterol	0
Fat	trace		

BROCCOLI FLORENTINE

2 packages (10 oz. each) frozen chopped spinach
¾ cup boiling water
1¼ teaspoons Morton Lite Salt mixture

⅓ cup half-and-half
¼ cup sliced green onions
1 package (10 oz.) frozen broccoli spears

Crumb Topping:

¼ cup dry bread crumbs
¼ teaspoon Morton Lite Salt mixture

¼ teaspoon nutmeg
Few grains cayenne pepper
1 tablespoon vegetable oil

Cook spinach in ½ cup of boiling water with ½ teaspoon salt for 20 minutes. Drain well. In buttered, shallow 1½-quart casserole, mix together cooked spinach, half-and-half, green onions and ½ teaspoon of salt. Set aside.

Cook broccoli in ¼ cup of boiling water with ¼ teaspoon salt for about 8 minutes, or until tender. Arrange broccoli spears over top of spinach mixture. (This much may be done ahead and refrigerated until shortly before serving.)

To make Crumb Topping: In a small bowl, combine crumbs, salt, nutmeg and cayenne. Mix well. Add oil, mix to moisten all the crumbs. Sprinkle over broccoli. Bake at 400° for 5 minutes (if at room temperature), for 10 to 15 minutes (if chilled), just until spinach bubbles and topping is browned. Makes 6 servings.

Per Serving

Calories	71	Sodium	368 mg.
Carbohydrate	10 Gm.	Potassium	626 mg.
Protein	5 Gm.	Cholesterol	7 mg.
Fat	2 Gm.		

BRUSSELS SPROUTS

Choose firm, solid, round heads with compact leaves and a fresh green color. Avoid yellow mottling. Cut off stem ends and remove wilted leaves. Cut a gash in each stem. Soak in water containing 2 tablespoons of Morton Lite Salt mixture for 30 minutes. Drain and rinse. Place in saucepan with 1 inch of boiling water containing ½ teaspoon of Morton Lite Salt mixture per pound. Without covering, cook for 3 minutes. Cover and cook for 8 to 15 minutes more. Drain. Serve with unsalted polyunsaturated margarine and lemon juice. One quart of sprouts serves 6.

Per Serving

Calories	34	Sodium	102 mg.
Carbohydrate	6 Gm.	Potassium	300 mg.
Protein	3 Gm.	Cholesterol	0
Fat	trace		

BRUSSELS SPROUTS AMANDINE

Cook 1 pint of sprouts as above. During the last 10 minutes of cooking, melt 2 tablespoons of unsalted polyunsaturated margarine in a heavy pan. Add ½ cup of shredded blanched almonds and shake over low heat until lightly browned. Drain sprouts, put in serving dish and top with almond mixture. If desired, sprinkle with a few drops of lemon juice. Makes 4 servings.

Per Serving

Calories	193	Sodium	9 mg.
Carbohydrate	9 Gm.	Potassium	400 mg.
Protein	7 Gm.	Cholesterol	0
Fat	18 Gm.		

CABBAGE

Choose a solid head, heavy for its size, with fresh leaves. Remove damaged outer leaves. Submerge in water and wash thoroughly. (If desired, add 2 tablespoons of Morton Lite Salt mixture to water.) To cook, cut into 6 to 8 wedges. Place in saucepan with 1 inch of boiling water and 1 teaspoon of Morton Lite Salt mixture. Cover and boil rapidly for 10 to 15 minutes, lifting cover from time to time. Or, for shredded cabbage, cut into thin strips with sharp French chef's knife or grater. Place in saucepan with 1 inch of boiling water and 1 teaspoon of Morton Lite Salt mixture. Cover and cook for 8 to 10 minutes or until tender. Drain. Add unsalted polyunsaturated margarine. Or dress with a small amount of vinegar. One pound serves 4.

Per Serving

Calories	27	Sodium	297 mg.
Carbohydrate	6 Gm.	Potassium	100 mg.
Protein	1 Gm.	Cholesterol	0
Fat	trace		

CHINESE-STYLE CABBAGE

3 tablespoons vegetable oil	1 teaspoon Morton Lite Salt mixture
5 cups (about 1 lb.) shredded cabbage	Dash pepper
2 tablespoons sugar	1 tablespoon white vinegar

Use a wok (a Chinese cooking pan), an electric skillet set to high, or a conventional skillet over high heat. Place oil in pan and heat. Add cabbage and reduce heat to moderate. Cook for 3 minutes, tossing and turning cabbage constantly. Add sugar, salt, pepper and vinegar. Cook, stirring constantly, until cabbage is crisp-tender (about 3 minutes). Reduce heat, cover and simmer for another 3 minutes. Makes 4 servings.

Per Serving

Calories	148	Sodium	300 mg.
Carbohydrate	13 Gm.	Potassium	450 mg.
Protein	2 Gm.	Cholesterol	0
Fat	11 Gm.		